Washington

for Children

Washington
for Children

A Comprehensive Guide to the
Unusual, Offbeat, and Exciting
In and Around Washington, for
Young People, Families, and Teachers

by Ray Shaw

CHARLES SCRIBNER'S SONS · NEW YORK

Library of Congress Cataloging in Publication Data

Shaw, Ray.
  Washington for children.

  1. Washington, D.C., region—Description and
travel—Guide-books.   I. Title.
F192.3.S45   917.53'04'4   74-16357
ISBN 684-14023-3

1 3 5 7 9 11 13 15 17 19 C/C 20 18 16 14 12 10 8 6 4 2
3 5 7 9 11 13 15 17 19 C/P 20 18 16 14 12 10 8 6 4 2

Printed in the United States of America

Dedication

To all who helped make Washington
the most important Capital in the world
and to my hungry-eyed young friends
who find such delight in my searching
and discovering the unusual
in and around Washington.

In Acknowledgment

I am especially grateful to Rich Hickman and John Phillips of the Washington Area Convention & Visitors Bureau for their assistance; and last, though not least, I wish to thank my editor, Harris Dienstfrey, for his enthusiasm and encouragement.

Contents

INTRODUCTION

Washington can be overwhelming. There is probably more to see here than in any other place in the world.

Washington is more than a city. It is the capital of the United States and the most visited seat of any government. Here is where our laws are passed and our history is made. It is the living showcase of our nation's heritage, of all we have struggled to create and sworn to uphold. Washington is the symbol of the American experience.

In *Washington for Children* we have attempted to outline the highlights, delights, and sidelights of the capital and its neighboring areas.

We have tried to avoid the obvious and familiar, though we have included a number of the popular attractions. In the main, we have concentrated on discovering the unusual, the offbeat, the things that call forth a reaction like: "I never would have believed *this* was in Washington!" Yet there it is, and here it is, presented for your enjoyment and enlightenment.

Don't try to see everything in this book in one visit. Spend time in each place you go, and make a note of the things you have missed or want to see again. Then include them in your next exciting trip to Washington.

To make certain our selection would have appeal to children, we escorted boys and girls of varying ages on trips. Their reaction and excitement helped determine the choice of a large number of the entries in this book.

To help you in planning your trip, we have included an index which lists the entries alphabetically.

A Note on the Smithsonian:

Since many of the entries are exhibits and displays in the Smithsonian, we will take a moment to explain that institution here.

James Smithson, a British scientist who never visited the United States, left a gift of $550,000 to found in Washington an institution for the "increase and diffusion of knowledge among men."

A building bearing his name, known as the "castle," was completed in Washington's southwest in 1858. Today the Smithsonian Institution is a complex of museums, art galleries, scientific and research centers, and it is ever-growing.

It is *not* part of our government, but it is under the government's guardianship, with a Board of Regents that includes the Chief Justice and Vice President of the United States, three Senators, three Representatives, six private citizens, and a Secretary.

It is no longer the "attic of the nation," or its "dust bin," as it was often referred to in the past. Today its treasures are beautifully arranged and dramatically displayed. In addition, the Smithsonian offers lectures, children's theatre performances, puppet shows, competitions, demonstrations, the Annual Folk Festival each July, and other special events.

Six million people from the United States and many parts of the world come each year to visit the many buildings and exhibits of the Smithsonian.

We have taken children of varying ages, at different times, to the Smithsonian exhibits and to the Zoo. Some of the visits included here are the ones the youngsters enjoyed the most, and the largest number wanted to go back and see them again.

Each Smithsonian gallery and museum has its own information service. For details about films, lectures, demonstrations, seminars, and other events, call the central information desk at 381-6264, or write the Office of Public Affairs, Smithsonian Institution, Washington, D.C. 20560. For ticket information call 381-5395.

Recorded Information:
Dial-A-Museum (737-8811) for exhibits and special events.
Dial-A-Phenomenon (737-8855) for weekly announcements on planets, stars, and worldwide occurrences.

Fossil Hunters:
Call Smithsonian Associates at 381-5157 for field trips in fossil hunting.

The following Smithsonian galleries and museums are included in this book.

1. National Air and Space Museum. This museum occupies the Arts and Industries Building, 900 Jefferson Drive, S.W., and the temporary quonset-type Air and Space Building nearby. The new Air and Space Museum now under construction on the mall between 4th and 7th Streets, S.W., will open July 4, 1976.

2. National Collection of Fine Arts
   8th and G Streets, N.W.

3. National Portrait Gallery
   F and 8th Streets, N.W.

4. Museum of Natural History
   10th & Constitution Avenue, N.W.

5. Museum of History and Technology
   14th & Constitution Avenue, N.W.

6. National Zoological Park
   3000 Block on Connecticut Avenue, N.W.

The above galleries and museums except the Zoo are open daily from 10:00–5:30. The following also have an expanded summer schedule from April 1 through Labor Day: the Air & Space Museum, Natural History, and History and Technology will be open 10:00 A.M.–9:00 P.M. The gates of the National Zoological Park open 6:00 A.M., buildings are open 9:00–4:30 in winter and until 6:30 in summer.

Highlight tours are conducted in some of the museums. Call 381-6264 about the different tours and schedules.

For school tours to the National Air and Space Museum, the Natural History and the Museum of History and Technology, write to School Services, Room 44, National Museum of Natural History, Smithsonian Institution, Washington, D.C. 20560.

For tours through the National Collection of Fine Arts and the National Portrait Gallery write to the respective museums, care of their Education Office.

1 **For Your Information**

MAP LEGEND

1. Union Station & National Visitors Center
2. Public Citizen Visitors Center
3. Travelers Aid Society
4. International Visitors Information Service
5. Washington Metropolitan Area Transit Authority
6. American University
7. Catholic University
8. Gallaudet College
9. Georgetown University
10. Howard University
11. University of Maryland
12. Fletcher's Boat House
13. Jack's Boats
14. Tow Path Cycle

HOW WASHINGTON IS DIVIDED

George Washington appointed a French engineer and a major in the Continental Army, Pierre Charles L'Enfant, to plan our capital.

L'Enfant envisioned Washington as the most elegant and spacious seat of government in the world, and planned the Capitol or "Presidential Palace" as the center of the city, with wide avenues radiating from it as from the hub of a wheel.

This is how Washington is laid out today: The Capitol is the nerve center, the focal point, and the area around it is divided into four somewhat uneven portions or quadrants. Roughly, the Northeast and Southeast are residential areas; the Southwest houses many government buildings and dwellings; and the Northwest is commercial and residential.

HOW WASHINGTON IS GOVERNED

Washington is the seat of our national government and a thriving community, but it is governed unlike any other community in the United States.

The Constitution states that Congress shall have the power to "exercise exclusive legislation . . . over . . . the seat of the Government of the United States . . ."

Originally the District, as it is often referred to, was governed by three commissioners appointed by the President. The people who lived here had neither the right to vote in national elections nor a voice in making the laws of the area. In 1961 the 23rd Amendment, for the first time, gave the residents the right to vote for a President. Then came the Reorganization of 1967, which called for the appointment by the President of a mayor and a nine-member council to govern the District.

In 1970 Congress approved legislation to have a delegate represent the District in the House of Representatives where he may vote on committees but not on the House Floor. The District does not have any Senators to represent it.

On May 7, 1974, the D.C. voters approved the Home Rule Referendum, and since January 1, 1975, Washington has had an elected mayor and city council. Congress, however, continues to retain its power over the District's budget.

POPULATION

The population of the District of Columbia proper is about 815,000, and it is estimated that by the year 2000 Metropolitan Washington, which includes nearby Maryland and Virginia, will grow to 5,000,000.

CLIMATE

Washington has a moderate climate and a reputation as the most "air-conditioned" city in the world.

For daily weather information dial WE6-1212.

The monthly high and low temperature averages are:

	JAN.	FEB.	MARCH	APRIL	MAY	JUNE
High	44	46	54	66	76	83
Low	30	29	36	46	56	65

	JULY	AUG.	SEPT.	OCT.	NOV.	DEC.
High	87	85	79	68	57	46
Low	69	68	61	50	39	31

BEFORE COMING TO WASHINGTON

The School Service Division of the Washington Area Convention and Visitors Bureau 1129 20th Street, N.W., Washington, D.C. 20036. Tel. (202) 659-6400,* offers suggestions to students and helps plan tours for out-of-town groups.

You may also want to write your Congressman to help arrange:

1. Foreign Policy Briefings in the State Department (See page 30)
2. VIP Tour to the White House (See page 32)
3. To obtain a flag flown over the Capitol (see below).

* The Washington telephone area code (202) will not be repeated in the text. The Maryland and Virginia area codes are listed, but many of the out of the District entries in the book are considered local calls. Ask your operator first or dial without the area code, and the operator will be sure to tell you if it is long distance.

Write your Congressman at least a month in advance of your visit. State exactly when you plan to arrive, the number of persons in your group, and what assistance you would like from his office.

To reach your Senator or Congressman by telephone, call him on the Capitol Switchboard number (224-3121). To write, address your Senator at the Senate Office Building and your Congressman at the House Office Building.

Don't hesitate to call on your legislators. They are happy to be of assistance to you. Visit your Congressman's office. Sign his guestbook, and if he isn't too busy he will chat with you, and may even pose for a picture with you on the Capitol steps.

The following material might also be useful:

Activities, an annual booklet published by the National Capital Park Service, 1100 Ohio Drive, S.W., Washington, D.C. 20042. Free.

Cultural Events Calendar (annual, free), and *Do You Know* (monthly, $1.00 a year), D.C. Recreation Department, 3149 16th Street, N.W., Washington, D.C. 20010.

Washington Area Convention and Visitors Bureau, 1129 20th Street, N.W., Washington, D.C. 20036. Request brochures on hotels, restaurants, and sightseeing tours.

A directory of sights and facilities especially prepared for handicapped persons on crutches or in wheelchairs, with warnings of narrow entrances, approaching steps, and cautions to cardiac patients of altitude changes, is also available. Write to the President's Committee on Employment of the Handicapped, Department of Labor Building, Washington, D.C. 20210. Free.

FLAGS OVER THE CAPITOL

If you want to bring back a memorable souvenir from Washington, order a flag that actually flew over the Capitol Building.

Flags come in two sizes, 3 × 5 and 5 × 8, and prices range from $2.60 to $6.00. Order them from your Congressman or Senator, but be sure to write him far in advance of your arrival, especially if you plan to visit Washington during the height of the tourist season.

A letter from the office of the Architect of the Capitol, with the date it was flown over the Capitol, will accompany your flag.

UNION STATION & NATIONAL VISITORS CENTER

The Union Station waiting room is the largest of its kind in the world. Resembling the baths of the Roman Emperor Diocletian, it is 220 feet long and 120 feet wide, with a 98-foot arched ceiling.

Above its six massive outside columns are 18-foot-high statues symbolizing Agriculture, Electricity, Fire, Freedom, Imagination and Mechanics. Among the inscriptions over the pavilion are:

1. "He that would bring home the wealth of the Indies must carry the wealth of the Indies with him. So it is with traveling—a man must carry knowledge with him if he would bring home knowledge."

2. "Let all the ends thou aimest at be thy country's . . . thy God's . . . and truth's."

3. "Welcome the coming, speed the departing guest."

The National Visitors Center is now under construction in the Union Station. Train schedules will go on uninterrupted, but part of the vast building will be devoted to the needs of many of the thirty million visitors expected during the Bicentennial Celebration.

The Center will include an information area, a hostel, an infirmary, nursery, theatres, translation facilities, a special programs room and other facilities that are still in the planning stages.

> Union Station
> Massachusetts & Delaware Avenues, N.E.
> Washington, D.C. 20009. Tel. 523-5300

PUBLIC CITIZEN VISITORS CENTER

Public Citizen Number One, Ralph Nader, has established the Public Citizen Visitors Center (PCVC) to encourage tourists to the nation's capital to find out how our government works. The Visitors Center is planning a diversified schedule of events which will include lectures and films, trips to government hearings, and face-to-face communications between the people and representatives of government agencies.

Since this is a new undertaking many changes and

refinements are expected to take place. Inquire about special interest tours and send a self-addressed, stamped envelope for its bi-weekly calendar.

Public Citizen Visitors Center
1200 15th Street, N.W.
Washington, D.C. 20005. Tel. 659-9053

All ages.   Individuals & groups.
Days & Hours: Monday–Friday 9–5. Saturday 10–1.
Admission: Free.
Guided Tour: On a limited basis. Telephone Fay Mauro, Direc-
tor, in advance.

TRAVELERS AID SOCIETY

The Travelers Aid Society is a national agency that assists children in transit and also travelers who have missed scheduled connections, lost their tickets or money, or need directions.

It also assists non-English-speaking travelers who have problems communicating in our language.

Travelers Aid representatives are stationed at the airports, bus terminals, and Union Station.

Emergency telephone service is available until 11 P.M.

Travelers Aid Society
1015 12th Street, N.W.
Washington, D.C. 20005. Tel. 347-0101

INTERNATIONAL VISITORS INFORMATION SERVICE

The International Visitors Information Service assists foreign guests with sightseeing plans, arranges visits with American families of similar interests or related professional affiliations, acts as interpreter, and sometimes even helps in obtaining lodging for foreign colleagues and their families.

International Visitors Information Service (IVS)
801 19th Street, N.W.
Washington, D.C. 20006. Tel. 347-4554

Days & Hours: Monday–Friday 9:30–5:30. Saturday 10:00–4:00
Closed Sunday and holidays.

HOW TO GET AROUND IN WASHINGTON

The fun way to get around in Washington is to walk, but many visitors have a limited time to spend here and must carefully budget their hours.

Whether you live in nearby Maryland or come from far away, make as many arrangements in advance as possible. Get a map of the city. Study it carefully.

Besides walking, you can get around by:

1. Bus

The District of Columbia has an extensive bus system with free transfers. Fare is 40 cents in *exact change.* Remember, bus drivers will not make change.

2. Taxi

Washington has more than 2,000 taxicabs. Fares are based on the zone system, and the city is divided into 8 taxi zones, beginning in the center of town and spreading outward:

Zone 1	*$ .85*	*5*	*$2.55*
2	*1.25*	*6*	*2.95*
3	*1.65*	*7*	*3.35*
4	*2.05*	*8*	*3.80*

3. Metro

Washington's first rail transit system is scheduled to open in 1975. It will combine the most distinctive features and conveniences of rail transit or subway systems around the world with the newest technology.

Guided tours will include subway-and-bus-related exhibits, repair shops, and other features still under construction.

Washington Metropolitan Area Transit Authority
600 Fifth Street, N.W.
Washington, D.C. 20001. Tel. 484-2633

Ages 7 and up.   Individuals & groups.
Days & Hours: *By appointment.*
Admission: *Free.*
Guided Tour: *Write or telephone at least one week in advance, Office, Director Community Services.*

4. Touring

Many touring facilities are also available. Among them:

a. *Sightseeing Buses* are listed in the Classified Directory of the Yellow Pages, or you may inquire at any hotel for information. Taxi drivers also take passengers on sightseeing tours. To avoid misunderstanding, arrange the fare in advance.

b. *Tourmobiles* are an inexpensive and convenient way of seeing the historic sites in and around Washington. An advantage of riding the Tourmobile is that you can get on and off as often as you wish, without paying extra fare. For ticket information and schedules, call 638-5371 or write Tourmobile Sightseeing Information, 900 Ohio Drive, S.W. Washington, D.C. 20024.

COLLEGES AND UNIVERSITIES

Washington's colleges and universities make the District of Columbia a major center of learning, and tours of campuses are offered by the schools. Some are guided tours, some are self-guided. Many include visits to classrooms, laboratories, galleries, sports events, TV and radio stations, and theatre rehearsals and productions.

For special visits, call or write the school directly:

1. American University
   Massachusetts & Nebraska Avenues, N.W.
   Washington, D.C. 20016. Tel. 338-7600

   Ages 12 and up.   Individuals & groups.
   Days & Hours: By appointment.
   Admission: Free.

Guided Tour: *Can be arranged. Write or telephone one week in advance.*

2. The Catholic University of America
   620 Michigan Avenue, N.E.
   Washington, D.C. 20017. Tel. 635-5600

   Ages 12 and up.   Groups only.
   Days & Hours: *By appointment.*
   Admission: *Free.*
   Guided Tour: *Can be arranged. Telephone two to three weeks in advance.*

   See entries under Nuclear Reactor, Glass Making, Tornadoes and Hurricanes.

3. Gallaudet College
   Florida Avenue & 7th Street, N.E.
   Washington, D.C. 20002. Tel. 447-0741

   Ages 10 and up.   Groups of 10–20 persons only.
   Days & Hours: *By appointment.*
   Admission: *Free.*
   Guided Tour: *Write or telephone Visitors Coordinator at least one week in advance.*

Students from many countries come to study at Gallaudet College, the world's only accredited liberal arts college for the deaf. It was founded in Washington in 1864 by an Act of Congress signed by Abraham Lincoln.

Whenever possible, tours are conducted by the students, and a visit includes the art department, an academic class, and a dance session or a play rehearsal when one is going on. All classes and activities are conducted in sign language. Arrangements may be made to see the closed circuit TV studio.

The students present major plays in sign language, with oral interpretation by off-stage readers. For information about performances and tickets, call the Drama Department, 447-0605.

4. Georgetown University
   37th & O Streets, N.W.
   Washington, D.C. 20007. Tel. 625-4866

   Ages 12 and up.   Individuals & groups.
   Days & Hours: Tours on weekdays at 10:30 A.M. and 3:30 P.M.
   Saturdays at 10:30 A.M.
   Admission: Free.
   Guided Tour: Groups should write or telephone in advance.

5. Howard University
   2400 6th Street, N.W.
   Washington, D.C. 20001. Tel. 636-6000

   Ages 12 and up.   Individuals & groups.
   Days & Hours: By appointment.
   Admission: Free.
   Guided Tour: Lasts about one hour. Write or telephone two
   weeks in advance.

6. University of Maryland
   College Park, Md. 20742. Tel. (301) 454-4104

   Ages 12 and up.   Individuals & groups.
   Days & Hours: By appointment.
   Admission: Free.
   Guided Tour: Write to Special Events, University Relations,
   University of Maryland.

HIKES AND BIKES

There are walking and bicycle trails through Rock Creek Park, along the Potomac River, and in other areas. For general information check with the National Capital Parks (426-6700). For up-to-the-minute information call 426-6975.

Bikes may be rented at:

Fletcher's Boat House, 4940 Canal Road, N.W., 244-0461

Jack's Boats, 3500 K Street, N.W., 337-9642

Tow Path Cycle, 2816 Pennsylvania Avenue, N.W., 337-7356

To bicycle owners: Register your two-wheeler at any Fire Department or Police Station, Monday through Saturday, 8 A.M.–8 P.M. For additional information or to report a lost or stolen bicycle call 626-2761.

INSTANT INFORMATION

Ambulance: Dial 911
* Dentist: Dental Referral Service, 541-4413
* Doctor: D.C. Medical Society Referral Service, 223-2200
Fire Department: 911
* Legal Aid: Lawyer Referral Service, 223-1484
Pharmacy (Open all night):

* These are referral numbers. You must call to make your own appointment.

Drug Fair, 17th & K Streets, N.W.
People's Drug Store, 14th St. & Mass. Ave., N.W.
Police: 911
Post Office (Open all night):
Mass. Avenue & N. Capitol St.
Time: Dial 844-2525
Weather: WE6-1212

For additional medical information: Many hotels have house physicians, and hospitals have emergency rooms.

For tourist information, call the Washington Area Convention and Visitors Bureau, 1129 20th Street, N.W., Washington, D.C. 20036. Tel. 659-6400.

DO YOU KNOW?

1. The original architect of the Capitol Building was William Thornton, a physician of English parentage, born on Tortola Island in the British West Indies.

2. George Washington is the only President who never lived in the White House. He selected the site and laid the cornerstone for the Executive Mansion in 1792, but he died in 1799. The White House was completed in 1800.

3. The White House was originally called the "President's Palace."

4. In 1814 the British partially burned the "Palace," and when it was rebuilt the outside was painted white to cover the soot and smoke that remained from the fire, and people began to refer to it as the "White House."

5. Our seventh President, Andrew Jackson, was the first

to have running water installed in the Executive Mansion in 1834.

6. The White House was lit by candles until 1848. Gaslight was installed during President James Knox Polk's administration.

7. A hot water system was first installed in the White House in 1853. Until then servants would carry buckets of heated water to prepare the President's bath.

8. An elevator was installed in the White House in the 1880s, during President Chester A. Arthur's term of office.

9. The White House was first lit by electricity in 1892, during President Benjamin Harrison's administration.

10. The 555-foot high Washington Monument is the tallest masonry structure in the world. It took forty years to build it (1848–88), and it takes 10 seconds by elevator to reach the top.

11. The Lincoln Memorial is surrounded by 36 marble columns, each representing a state in the Union at the time of President Lincoln's death. Fifty-six steps, one for each year of Lincoln's life, lead to the place where the statue stands.

WHAT'S THE TIME?

When it's 12 noon in Washington, it is:

Anchorage, Alaska	7:00 A.M.
Atlanta, Ga.	12:00 Noon
Boston, Mass.	12:00 Noon

Chicago, Ill.	11:00 A.M.
Cleveland, Ohio	12:00 Noon
Dallas, Tex.	11:00 A.M.
Denver, Col.	10:00 A.M.
Detroit, Mich.	12:00 Noon
Honolulu, Hawaii	7:00 A.M.
Kansas City, Mo.	11:00 A.M.
Los Angeles, Cal.	9:00 A.M.
Milwaukee, Wis.	11:00 A.M.
New Orleans, La.	11:00 A.M.
New York City	12:00 Noon
San Francisco, Cal.	9:00 A.M.
Seattle, Wash.	9:00 A.M.
St. Louis, Mo.	11:00 A.M.

BICENTENNIAL

Thirty million visitors, many of them from far-away places, are expected to come to Washington to share in the celebration of the founding of America and to be part of the excitement our 200th anniversary will generate. For information communicate with:

Office of Communications
American Revolution Bicentennial Administration
736 Jackson Place, N.W.
Washington, D.C. 20276. Tel. 254-5567

2 Government

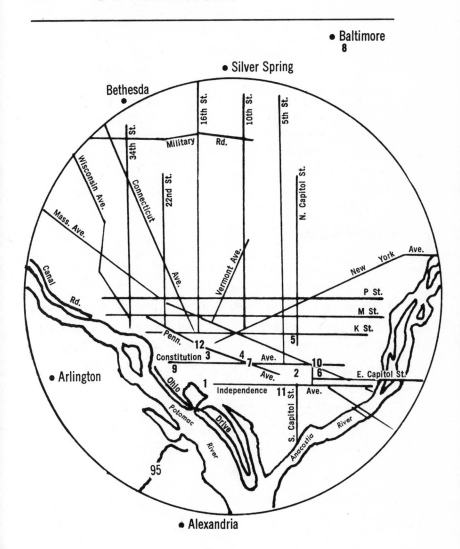

MAP LEGEND

1. Bureau of Engraving and Printing
2. Capitol
3. Department of Commerce
4. FBI
5. Government Printing Office
6. Library of Congress
7. National Archives
8. Social Security Administration
9. State Department
10. Supreme Court
11. Voice of America
12. White House

BUREAU OF ENGRAVING AND PRINTING

The Bureau of Engraving and Printing is part of the Treasury Department, and is the largest printing house of its kind in the world.

From a glass-enclosed gallery, visitors listen to recorded descriptions of the printing operations they watch in front of them.

Fifty million dollars are printed every day in $1, $5, and $10 denominations. The $20 bills are printed less often, and $50s and $100s are printed once a year. The $500, $1,000, $5,000, and $10,000 bills have not been produced since 1945.

Secret formula ink and specially made cotton and linen paper are used so as to discourage counterfeiters.

The Bureau of Engraving and Printing produces only our paper money. The Bureaus of the Mint in Philadelphia and Denver produce our coin money.

For never-before-touched coins and just-printed paper currency, visit the Treasury Department's Cash Room at Pennsylvania Avenue and 15th Street, N.W., Washington, D.C. 20220.

Bureau of Engraving & Printing
14th & C Streets, S.W.
Washington, D.C. 20228. Tel. 964-7873

All ages.　Individuals & groups.
Days & Hours: Monday–Friday 8:00–2:30. Closed holidays.
Admission:　Free.
Guided Tour:　Not available.

CAPITOL

The United States Capitol, where our 100 Senators and 435 Representatives meet to make our laws, is one of the most imposing and popular sights in Washington.

Both Chambers of Congress have visitors' galleries. To obtain a pass of admittance, contact your Senator or Congressman.

The offices of the Senators and Representatives are located not in the Capitol itself, but in five nearby office buildings. All legislators can be reached by calling the Capitol Switchboard at 224-3121.

The two Senate Office Buildings are connected to the Capitol by a miniature underground train, known as the Senate Subway. The free ride, a favorite with youngsters, covers a distance of 892 feet and it takes 52 seconds to make the journey.

United States Capitol
Capitol Hill
Washington, D.C. 20515. Tel. 224-3121

All ages.   Individuals & groups.
Days & Hours: Daily 9:00–4:30. Closed Thanksgiving, Christmas, New Year's.
Admission: Free.
Guided Tour: Around every 15 minutes in the winter, every 5 minutes during the summer. Last tour starts at 3:45.

DEPARTMENT OF COMMERCE BUILDING

The U.S. Department of Commerce Building has three permanent attractions of interest to visitors:

1. The huge census clock in the lobby with its every tick records our births, deaths, immigration, and emigration, and gives us at a glance the estimated total population of the United States.

2. The seismograph, an apparatus that records earthquakes, is located nearby on the lobby floor.

3. The National Aquarium is on the floor below. See Aquarium, Chapter 9 (page 161).

U.S. Department of Commerce Building
14th Street and Constitution Avenue, N.W.
Washington, D.C. 20230. Tel. 967-2825

All ages.   Individuals & groups.
Days & Hours: Open daily 9:00–5:00. Closed Christmas.
Admission: Free.
Guided Tour: Not available.

FBI

A guided tour of the FBI headquarters, a part of the Justice Department, is an unforgettable experience in every young visitor's life. But old as well as young enjoy these tours.

More than 3,000 persons a day are guided through the FBI laboratory section and see agents studying blood samples, poisons, fabrics, or car paints as they look for clues to solve crimes. More than 159,000,000 fingerprints on file aid the investigators in identifying and apprehending criminals.

The tour guide, either a college student or Special Agent, explains the work of the department, and an expert demonstrates the firing of weapons at the indoor range. Later, the tour group passes the hall of infamous criminals, which includes the "ten most wanted men."

Federal Bureau of Investigation
9th and Pennsylvania Avenue, N.W.
Washington, D.C. 20535. Tel. 393-7100

All ages. Individuals & groups.
Days & Hours: Monday–Friday 9:15–4:15.
Admission: Free.
Guided Tour: Hour tours every 15 minutes. Groups of more than 15 persons should write or telephone in advance.

GOVERNMENT PRINTING OFFICE

The United States Government Printing Office is the world's largest printing plant. Each year 7,000 employees, occupying four buildings on 33 acres of land, produce billions of documents.

Tours are *not* available to the general public. Only graphic arts and library science students from junior high school and up and people in the writing field, in other government agencies, or those associated with graphic arts or libraries are welcome.

For a monthly free listing of current publications, write to:

Superintendent
U.S. Government Printing Office
710 North Capitol Street, N.W.
Washington, D.C. 20401. Tel. 541-3000

Ages 12 and up.   Groups only.
Days & Hours: *By appointment.*
Admission: Free.
Guided Tour: *Tour is limited to special groups. Lasts about 2 hours. Write in advance, giving the number in your group.*

LIBRARY OF CONGRESS

The Library of Congress is a vital part of our national heritage.

It began with the purchase of Thomas Jefferson's 6,487-volume library for $24,000. Today it is the largest library in the world, containing 320 miles of bookshelves. Its over 85 million articles include more than 16 million books, 3 million items of music, and a collection of rare musical instruments, including some by Stradivarius.

Originally established as a reference law library for the members of Congress, it now serves all branches of our government, and also other libraries and scholars. It is open as well to researchers.

Many important historic documents are preserved here. They include Jefferson's handwritten draft of the Declaration of Independence, Lincoln's Gettysburg Address, and treasures of early printing. One of the library's most valuable possessions is an original copy of the Gutenberg Bible. The library bought it in 1930, reportedly for $300,000.

A list of Library of Congress Publications in Print is available free through the Central Service Division. A Calendar of Events is also available upon request.

Library of Congress
10 First Street, S.E.
Washington, D.C. 20540. Tel. 426-5000

Ages 10 and up.   Individuals & groups.
Days & Hours: Monday–Saturday 8:30 A.M.–9:30 P.M. Sunday
11:00 A.M.–9:30 P.M. Closed Christmas.
Admission: Free.
Guided Tour: Every hour 9:00–4:00 Monday–Friday. For group
tours, write or telephone Brian Willson, Tour
Coordinator, Tel. 426-5458.

NATIONAL ARCHIVES

The most important documents of our nation—the Declaration of Independence, the Constitution, and the Bill of Rights—are preserved and exhibited in the National Archives.

The bronze doors that guard these national treasures

are reputed to be the largest in the world, and the burglar alarm system is considered one of the most efficient ever devised.

Exhibits of other historic documents, paintings, and maps are also displayed.

The National Archives
Constitution Avenue between 7th & 9th Sts., N.W.
Washington, D.C. 20408. Tel. 963-6404

Ages 10 and up.   Individuals & groups.
Days & Hours: Monday–Saturday 9:00 A.M.–10:00 P.M. Sunday 1:00–10:00. Closes at 6 in winter. Closed Christmas and New Year's.
Admission: *Free.*
Guided Tour: *For groups and families only. Write or telephone two weeks in advance.*

POSTAL SERVICE

The U.S. Postal Service has recently organized a program for students, grades three to twelve, offering information about our postal system, which is as old as our country. The story of our mail system is fascinating and full of little known facts:

Benjamin Franklin was our first Postmaster General, Abraham Lincoln was postmaster of New Salem, Illinois. The first letter to travel by air was written by George Washington and carried on January 9, 1793, by balloon from Philadelphia, then the nation's capital, to a stump-filled clearing in the woods of Deptford, New Jersey.

For information about the program communicate with:

U.S. Postal Service
Room 10941
475 L'Enfant Plaza, S.W.
Washington, D.C. 20024. Tel. 245-4112

Ages 8 and up.

At this postal service office, the Philatelic Sales and Exhibition Room will have display cases of commemorative, historic, and current United States stamps and a large selection of unusual foreign ones, many for sale. Beginning in November 1976, the display will be open Monday–Saturday 8:15–4:45. Closed holidays. No guided tours, but visitors will be welcome to browse to their hearts' content. For additional information telephone 245-4000.

SOCIAL SECURITY

You don't have to be grandma's age to visit the Social Security Administration Office. Young people should also become acquainted with its program.

Groups of fifty or more, of all ages, tour the building and learn how the earnings of 250,000,000 people are programmed by electronic data processing equipment. They also see how the monthly benefits of 30,000,000 former wage-earners are computed and sent to retirees all over the world.

The tour concludes with the showing of a film on social security, followed by a question-and-answer session.

Social Security Administration (40 miles from D.C.)
6401 Security Blvd.
Baltimore, Md. 21235. Tel. (301) 594-2374

Ages 12 and up.   Individuals & groups.
Days & Hours: Monday–Friday 9:30–2:00.
Admission: Free.
Guided Tour: Lasts 1½ hours, but allow 2½ hours for complete program. Write or telephone one week in advance.

STATE DEPARTMENT

1. Guided Tour
The State Department conducts daily tours to its International Conference Room where the Secretary of State meets the press and to the Diplomatic Reception Rooms where foreign dignitaries are received.

U.S. State Department
2201 C Street, N.W.
Washington, D.C. 20520. Tel. 632-3241

Ages 15 and up.
Groups only, but individuals may join scheduled tour.
Days & Hours: Monday–Friday 9:30, 10:30, and 3:30.
Admission: Free.

Guided Tour: *Write or telephone 2 to 3 weeks in advance, or ask your Congressman's office to make arrangements for you.*

2. Briefings

A short, twice-weekly briefing not necessarily on designated days gives one some idea how our diplomatic machinery works. These talks are of particular interest to high school students who are thinking of specializing in government, international relations, and world affairs.

Make your own arrangements. Write or telephone 632-2406, or ask your Congressman's office to make arrangements for you.

SUPREME COURT

The dazzling white, classic Greek building with its gracefully ornate columns is the highest court in the land.

The Supreme Court is made up of a Chief Justice and eight Associate Justices often referred to as the "nine old men." They constitute our government's Judiciary Department and are appointed to serve for life terms during good behavior. Their function is to interpret our laws independent of Congress, the President, and the voters.

Since the founding of our country there have been a hundred justices in all, fifteen Chief Justices and eighty-five Associates.

The Supreme Court Building is open to visitors all year, but the Court is in session only eight months, from October through May. Check for the exact dates that the Court is in session.

Supreme Court of the United States
1 First Street, N.E.
Washington, D.C. 20543. Tel. 393-1640

All ages but of greater interest to older children.
Individuals & groups.
Days & Hours: *Monday–Friday 9:00–4:30. Closed holidays.*
Admission: *Free.*
Guided Tour: *A short guided tour on a first-come basis is available Monday–Friday 9:30–4:00, except when Court is in session. To check Court schedule call the Marshal's office or dial 639-0220 for recorded information.*

VOICE OF AMERICA

The United States Information Agency, of which the Voice of America is a branch, explains us—you, me, and our government—to the peoples of the world.

The Voice broadcasts 858 hours a week by short and medium wave in 36 languages. It reaches an estimated audience of 50 million persons over the age of 14 through its 189 posts in 100 foreign countries.

The Voice also produces and acquires over 500 films and TV documentaries each year, seen by an estimated billion and a half people.

On your tour you will see the workings of a radio station and you will learn how programs are produced and recorded.

The exhibits on the walls describe the activities of the USIA around the world.

Voice of America
330 Independence Avenue, S.W.
Washington, D.C. 20547. Tel. 755-4744

Ages 14 and up.   Individuals & groups up to 20 persons.
Days & Hours: Monday–Friday 9:00–4:00 except 12:00–1:00.
Admission: Free.
*Guided Tour: A 45-minute tour every hour on the hour except
                between 12:00–1:00. For group tour telephone in
                advance.*

WHITE HOUSE AND VIP TOUR

A special White House visit known as the VIP Tour is available to early birds. These year-round visits begin between 8:00 and 8:30 on those mornings that the White House is open to tourists.

Since the number of persons on these visits is limited, it is advisable to make arrangements far in advance. Write your Congressman to help make reservations for you. Be sure to indicate the date of your arrival in Washington. Notify his office if there is any change in your plans, and check with his secretary when you arrive in town.

In addition to the VIP Tour, the White House is open to the public.

The White House
1600 Pennsylvania Avenue, N.W.
Washington, D.C. 20500. Tel. 456-1414

All ages.   Individuals & groups.

Days & Hours: Tuesday–Saturday 10:00–12. Open Saturday until 2:00 during June, July, and August. Closed holidays.

Admission: Free.

Guided Tour: Not available, but stationed guards answer questions. For additional information call Visitors Office.

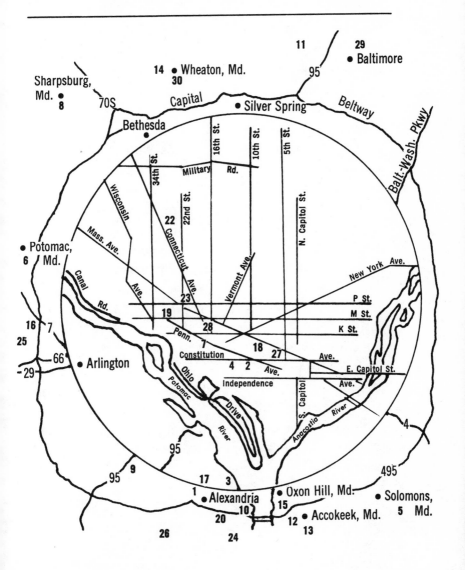

MAP LEGEND

1. Alexandria
2. Smithsonian Museum of Natural History
3. Stabler-Leadbeater Apothecary
4. Smithsonian Museum of History and Technology
5. Calvert Maritime Museum
6. Chesapeake & Ohio Canal Park
7. Daughters of the American Revolution
8. Antietam National Battlefield
9. Fort Ward Museum & Park
10. Gadsby's Tavern
11. Carroll County Farm Museum
12. Alice Ferguson Foun.
13. National Colonial Farm
14. Old MacDonald's Farm
15. Oxon Hill Children's Farm
16. Turkey Run Farm
17. Friendship Veterans Fire Engine Co.
18. Ford's Theatre and Lincoln Museum
19. Old Stone House
20. George Washington's Grist Mill
21. Langrell's Mill
22. Pierce Mill
23. Anderson House Museum
24. Gunston Hall Plantation
25. Sully Plantation
26. Woodlawn Plantation
27. Smithsonian National Portrait Gallery
28. National Rifle Association Firearms Museum
29. Star-Spangled Banner Flag House
30. National Capital Trolley Museum

ALEXANDRIA—"The Old Town"

Situated on the Potomac River, south of Washington, Alexandria was founded in 1749 and flourished as a busy tobacco-shipping center in its early days.

Many of the historic places in this book are located in and around Alexandria, and for those who wish to recapture the spirit of our country's early history, a visit to the city is recommended, especially to its "Old Town."

Here one sees the Georgian-style Christ Church where our first President served as vestryman, the Stabler-Leadbeater Apothecary Shop, the Friendship Veterans Fire Engine Company, and Gadsby's Tavern where our first President made his headquarters during the French and Indian War and where he attended his last birthday celebration February 22, 1799.

Not to be missed are the rows of quaint old houses on historic cobblestoned Prince Street paved by Hessian soldiers during the 1780s.

For information and tours about historic Alexandria, communicate with:

Alexandria Tourist Council
221 King Street
Alexandria, Va. 22314. Tel. (703) 549-0206

AMERICAN INDIANS

The Smithsonian Museum of Natural History has displays on the history, life, arts, and crafts of the American

Indian. The exhibits highlight some of the contributions made by the many Indian tribes of North, Central, and South America, and include a model Pueblo village, Navajo crafts, and Hopi snake dancers. The exhibit of totem poles is particularly interesting.

The totem poles originally had a mystical and spiritual significance, and the American Indians of the West Coast designed and built the most colorful and artistic of these poles and set them upright in front of their dwellings.

Examples of the huge, colorful totem poles stand majestically inside the entrance to the Natural History Museum and attract the visiting youngsters who love to crawl inside their bases.

- At the Smithsonian Museum of Natural History.

APOTHECARY SHOPS

George Washington, Robert E. Lee, Daniel Webster, and other famous Americans were regular customers here.

Now a museum, this apothecary shop, which was founded in 1792, remained in business until 1933, and was operated throughout its history by a member of the Leadbeater family.

The shop doesn't look much different today from the way it did when our first President filled his prescriptions here. Original pharmacist's tools, handblown glass containers, jars, and furnishings have all been preserved.

Stabler-Leadbeater Apothecary (7 miles from D.C.)

105 S. Fairfax Street
Alexandria, Va. 22314. Tel. 863-3717

All ages.   Individuals & groups.
Days & Hours: Monday–Saturday 10:00–12:00 & 1:30–5:00.
Admission: Voluntary contribution optional.
Guided Tour: Not available.

The Smithsonian's Hall of Pharmacy is also a fascinating place. It contains an 18th-century European apothecary and an American pharmacy of the 1880s, a collection of druggist's tools, jars, and containers as well as information explaining the origin of drugs and the development of antibiotics.
• At the Smithsonian Museum of History and Technology.

CALVERT MARITIME MUSEUM

The Calvert Maritime Museum has a fine collection of model boats, fossils, and memorabilia dating back to the days when the Chesapeake Bay was an important seafaring area.

Calvert Maritime Museum (65 miles from D.C.)
P.O. Box 44
Solomons, Md. 20688. Tel. (301) 326-3107

All ages.   Individuals & groups.
Days & Hours: Saturdays and Sundays all year 1:00–5:00. School groups are welcome on weekdays by appointment.

Admission: *Voluntary contribution.*
Guided Tour: *For school groups during weekdays, by appointment.*

CANDY SHOP

A fully-equipped confectionery shop that did a flourish-
ing business in Georgetown seventy-five years ago now
stands in the Museum of History and Technology.

The model stick candy looks so real you can almost
smell it.

• At the Smithsonian Museum of History and Technology.

CHESAPEAKE & OHIO CANAL

The Chesapeake and Ohio Canal, built before the Civil
War, is now a national historic landmark.

Used commercially until 1924, the canal begins in
Georgetown and continues to Cumberland, Maryland, 185
miles from Washington.

Nature trails, a gold mine, historic and environmental
hikes, lectures and movies about the canal are available.
For information about boating, camping, canoeing, and
hiking contact the National Park Service 299-3613.

Due to the 1972 hurricane the famous barge trips on the
canal had to be discontinued, but they may be resumed at
some future time.

The Great Falls Tavern, built in 1830, is now a visitors'
center and houses a museum on the history of the canal.

Chesapeake & Ohio Canal Park (10 miles from D.C.)
11710 MacArthur Blvd.
Potomac, Md. 20854. Tel. (301) 299-3613

All ages.   Individuals & groups.
Days & Hours: Museum open all year. Winter, 9:00–5:00. Summer, 9:00–8:00. Closed Christmas.
Admission: Free.
Guided Tour: By appointment.

CHILDREN OF THE AMERICAN REVOLUTION

Fascinating to all visitors—though of special appeal to little girls—is the dollhouse, the doll collection, and the schoolbooks used by children of our pioneers, all exhibited at the National Society of Daughters of the American Revolution.

In addition, there is an exhibit of twenty-eight handsomely furnished rooms, designed by outstanding craftsmen of each of the twenty-eight states represented, that tell the story of regional America.

Daughters of the American Revolution
1776 D Street, N.W.
Washington, D.C. 20006. Tel. 628-4980, Ext. 254 or 292

Ages 4 and up.   Individuals & groups up to 50 persons.
Days & Hours: Monday–Friday 9:00–4:00. Closed holidays.
Admission: Free.
Guided Tour: By appointment. Telephone two weeks in advance.

CIVIL WAR BATTLEFIELD

The Antietam National Battlefield in Sharpsburg, Maryland, commemorates one of the important battles of the Civil War. Named after the nearby Antietam Creek, the battle marked Robert E. Lee's unsuccessful attempt to invade the North.

The tour includes battlefield sites, musket demonstrations, and audio-visual presentations.

> Antietam National Battlefield (70 miles from D.C.)
> P.O. Box 158
> Sharpsburg, Md. 21782. Tel. (301) 432-5142
>
> All ages.   Individuals & groups.
> *Days & Hours: Daily 8:30–5:00. Summer 8:00–6:00.*
> *Admission: Free.*
> *Guided Tour: Lasts about 2 hours. Write 2 weeks in advance.*

CIVIL WAR FORT AND MUSEUM

Fort Ward, a Civil War fort, was originally built to protect Washington, D.C. against invasion by the Confederate Army.

The fort has been partially rebuilt, and the museum, patterned after a Civil War photograph by Mathew Brady, portrays the history and displays uniforms, tools, firearms, and a variety of instruments of that period.

> Fort Ward Museum & Park
> 4301 W. Braddock Road

Alexandria, Va. 22304. Tel. (703) 750-6425

All ages. Individuals & groups.
Days & Hours: Monday–Saturday 9:00–5:00, Sunday 12:00–5:00.
Closed Thanksgiving & Christmas.

COLONIAL THEATRE

Late August through early September each year, a revival of colonial theatre is presented in the courtyard of historic Gadsby's Tavern by the Little Theatre of Alexandria. Performers and staff, including barmaids and innkeeper, all dress in Early American costumes. In addition, the tavern is open daily as a tourist attraction for those interested in Americana.

Gadsby's Tavern
128 N. Royal Street
Alexandria, Va. 22314. Tel. (703) 683-5564

All ages. Individuals & groups.
Days & Hours: The Tavern is open daily 10:00–5:00. For theatre performances consult newspapers or telephone 683-0496.
Admission: To the Tavern, children under 12 free. Adults $.25. For performances, including refreshments: $3.75.
Guided Tour: Not available. Reservation for performances see above.

COSTUMES AND GOWNS OF THE FIRST LADIES

The American Costume Collection reveals what women, and men too, wore as long ago as the pioneer days. Exhibits show the change of styles through the centuries: hemlines up and down, necklines high and low, and a vivid assortment of shoes, gloves, and other accessories.

A display of special interest contains the gowns worn by all the first ladies from Martha Washington to the present.

• At the Smithsonian Museum of History and Technology.

DENTIST'S OFFICE

All dentist-fearing children should see this office of a practicing dentist of 1895. One look at the chair, the early equipment, and the tools he used will make youngsters love the dentist back home.

An added bonus is a slide show of modern dental techniques and equipment. And no one should miss seeing our first President's gold and ivory false teeth.

• At the Smithsonian Museum of History and Technology.

FARM MUSEUM

The Carroll County Farm Museum, established in 1965, is Maryland's first agricultural museum.

Built on 142 acres of land, the museum contains an 1850 farm house, barn, smoke and spring houses, a blacksmith shop, carriages, wagons, early threshing machines, and one of the first wagons used in rural mail delivery.

Special demonstrations of broommaking, blacksmithing, spinning, pottery, candlemaking, and weaving are scheduled throughout the year.

Carroll County Farm Museum (50 miles from D.C.)
Route 6, Box 412
Westminster, Md. 21157. Tel. (301) 848-7775

All ages.   Individuals & groups.
Days & Hours: *Open weekends April–October 12:00–5:00. July and August, Tuesday–Sunday, 10:00–4:00. Other times by appointment.*
Admission: *Children 6–18: $.50. Adults: $1.50.*
Guided Tour: *By appointment. Write or telephone one week in advance.*

FARMS

1. Alice Ferguson Foundation

A fully operating farm on more than 250 acres of fertile land gives us a glimpse into a back-to-the-soil way of life. A visit here is a stimulating lesson in the study of our environment.

Animals are raised, crops are grown, and in all, the farm offers a rare opportunity to learn respect for nature and to gain an understanding of the need to preserve the natural balance of our world.

Open to scout groups and to local elementary school children, preferably from Southern Maryland's Prince George and Charles counties. Tours are occasionally scheduled for local high school ecology classes and for D.C. and Virginia groups.

Alice Ferguson Foundation, Inc. (14 miles from D.C.)
Route 1, Box 618
Accokeek, Md. 20607. Tel. (301) 283-2695

Ages 5–12.   Groups only.
Days & Hours: Monday–Friday   10:00–12:00.   By appointment only.
Admission: *Free.*
Guided Tour: *For elementary school groups only. Write or telephone for reservations.*

2. National Colonial Farm

The National Colonial Farm across the Potomac from Mt. Vernon is an authentic reconstruction of a small colonial farm, with dairy and beef cattle, horses, mid-eighteenth-century crops, and a medicinal and kitchen herb garden.

One thousand American chestnut seedlings have recently been planted here, and a historical agricultural museum is now under construction.

Young people from schools throughout the country come here to work the soil and to learn colonial farming methods.

National Colonial Farm (20 miles from D.C.)
Route 1, Box 697

Accokeek, Md. 20607. Tel. (301) 283-2113

Ages 11 and up.   Individuals & groups.
*Days & Hours: Daily June 1–Labor Day, 10:00–5:00. Other times
              by appointment.*
Admission: Children: $.25. Adults: $.50.
Guided Tour: Write or telephone in advance.

3. Old MacDonald's Farm

Old MacDonald's Farm is a typical Maryland farm in miniature, with all the animals in the famous children's song and more.

The barnyard is filled with chicks, ducklings, colts, and piglets. The grounds include a barn, a silo, a smokehouse, a bread oven, and a windmill.

Don't miss the nearby playground with a Navy jet fighter, the Wheaton Stage Coach, pony rides, and a two-mile trip on a replica of a colorful 1865 steam engine train.

Old MacDonald's Farm (4 miles from D.C.)
2000 Shorefield Road
Wheaton, Md. 20902. Tel: (301) 622-0056

All ages.   Individuals & groups.
Days & Hours: All year from 10:00 A.M. to sunset.
Admission: Free.
*Guided Tour: Not available. Groups arriving by bus should
              telephone 589-1480 in advance for a bus permit.*

4. Oxon Hill Children's Farm

Oxon Hill Children's Farm is typical of an American farm in this area at the turn of the century.

Chickens, cows, pigs, and horses wander on its 375 acres; assorted vegetables grow in the garden. Tourists may see demonstrations of farming practices and seasonal arts and crafts of the early 1900s—among them, wheat threshing, corn picking, molasses cooking, and sheep shearing.

Guides and farm workers in period costumes are available as escorts, but visitors may walk around on their own and pet the animals, watch the farmers at work, or even help with the harvesting.

Oxon Hill Children's Farm (on the outskirts of D.C.)
6411 Oxon Hill Road
Oxon Hill, Md. 20021. Tel. (301) 839-1177

All ages.   Individuals & groups.
Days & Hours: *October–May 8:00–5:00. June–September 8:00–7:00.*
Admission: *Free.*
Guided Tour: *For guided tour during the school year, write or telephone (301) 426-6921 one month in advance.*

5. Turkey Run Farm

A low-income homestead of the 1770s is re-created at Turkey Run Farm. Here you can see how a family lived on its land, tended livestock, planted fields, and cared for crops in colonial Virginia.

Turkey Run Farm (15 miles from D.C.)
McLean, Va. 22101. Tel. (703) 557-1357 / 3635

All ages.   Individuals & groups.
Days & Hours: Open Wednesday–Sunday 10:00–4:30. Winter: Friday–Sunday 10:00–4:30.

Admission: Free.
Guided Tour: For guided tours or large groups, write or tele-
                phone two months in advance.

FIRE HOUSE

President Washington, to whom firefighting was a passion, was an honorary member of the Friendship Veterans Fire Engine Company, organized in Alexandria in 1774. There is no record of his ever having assisted in extinguishing a fire.

In 1775, Washington donated a fire engine that he had purchased in Philadelphia for 80 pounds and 10 shillings —the equivalent of $400—and had it delivered to Alexandria by oxcart.

Other historic equipment on display is a horsedrawn fire engine, leather fire buckets, hatchets, helmets, and uniforms.

House plaques, still attached to the outside of some homes, were an indication that those residents contributed or volunteered in putting out fires in the community. Woe to the plaqueless when a fire broke out in their own homes.

Friendship Veterans Fire Engine Co. (7 miles from D.C.)
107 S. Alfred Street
Alexandria, Va. 22314. No telephone.

All ages.   Individuals & groups up to 40 persons.
Days & Hours: Monday–Saturday 10:00–4:00. Closed Sunday
              and in bad weather.

Admission: Free.
Guided Tour: Lasts about 20 minutes. Reservations not needed.

FORD'S THEATRE AND LINCOLN MUSEUM

Ford's Theatre, where Abraham Lincoln was shot on April 14, 1865, was restored in 1968.

The Presidential Box looks as it did the night President Lincoln was shot, with the stage set for *Our American Cousin*, the play he was watching. The museum in the basement displays objects our 16th President used in his private and public life.

During the day there are special talks on theatre, self-guiding tours to the Museum, and in the summer sound and light programs re-create the Civil War and the story of the assassination. There are also all-year-round theatre performances, including one-man shows, musicals, and contemporary dramas. For ticket information call 347-6260.

Ford's Theatre and Lincoln Museum
511 Tenth Street, N.W.
Washington, D.C. 20004. Tel. 638-2941

All ages.   Individuals & groups.
Days & Hours: Daily 9:00–5:00 for museum visitors; 7:30 for live performances. Closed Christmas and New Year's.
Admission: Free to visit the theatre and museum during the day, but there is a charge for performances.

Guided Tour: Large groups only may request a tour and
individuals may join a scheduled visit.

GEORGETOWN—"Old Stone House"

Georgetown was a thriving Virginia tobacco port in its
early days. Founded in 1665, it became a part of the
District of Columbia in 1878. Today part of it is an
exclusive residential area with tree-shaded streets, while
part is studded with boutiques, art galleries, and craft
shops.

One of the first dwellings built in Washington and the
oldest in Georgetown is the "Old Stone House." Con-
structed in 1765, and considered a fine example of
pre-Revolutionary architecture, it is an ever-popular site.

Visitors are guided through its rooms by colonial-
costumed ladies who demonstrate early American cook-
ery, spinning, weaving, candle-dipping, and pomander
ball-making.

Old Stone House
3051 M. Street, N.W.
Washington, D.C. 20851. Tel. 426-6851

All ages.   Individuals & groups.
Days & Hours: Daily 9:30–5:00. Closed Christmas and New
Year's.
Admission: Free.
Guided Tour: Large groups should write or telephone in ad-
vance.

MILITARY HISTORY

America's military and naval history from its beginning is exhibited in the Smithsonian's Armed Forces History Department.

Of great interest is George Washington's field headquarters tent with his four-poster bed, desk, and the general's jacket thrown over a nearby chair.

Another highlight is the intact wooden gunboat *Philadelphia,* sunk in battle on Lake Champlain in 1776 and retrieved with much of her equipment in 1936.

Uniforms, weapons, and flags are also on display.

• At the Smithsonian Museum of History and Technology.

MILLS

The mill played an important role in the life of our early settlers. Here the miller ground flour for his own needs, sold the surplus, and did the milling for other farmers. The going rate of payment during early colonial times was usually one-eighth of the flour milled.

The mill also served as a social center in the community. Not unlike the waterwell of ancient times, it was the gathering place where people would exchange news, discuss mutual problems, meet kinfolk, or trade gossip.

There are many early flour mills in the Washington area. Here we list only a few:

1. George Washington's Grist Mill

George Washington's Grist Mill was built in 1735, and was in working condition during most of our first President's life, including his eight years in office.

It deteriorated after he died, and in the 1930s it was restored as a tourist attraction by the Virginia Division of Parks, though not to full operating condition.

There is a display of old tools and mill machinery and a slide show explaining its history.

George Washington's Grist Mill (16 miles from D.C.)
5541 Mt. Vernon Memorial Highway
Alexandria, Va. 22309. Tel. (703) 780-3383

All ages.　Individuals & groups.
Days & Hours: *Open daily from Memorial Day through September, 10:00–6:00, and weekends during October, April, and May. Special visits may be arranged at other times.*
Admission: *Children: $.25. Adults: $.50.*
Guided Tour: *Large groups must write or telephone in advance.*

2. Langrell's Mill

Langrell's Mill, formerly Murray's Mill, located on Hunting Creek, is one of the oldest flour mills still in continuous service. Dating back to 1658, it helped supply flour to the Continental Army.

Langrell's Mill (80 miles from D.C.)
P.O. Box Preston
Linchester, Md. 21655. Tel. (301) 673-7613

All ages.   Individuals & groups.
*Days & Hours: Monday, Tuesday, Thursday, and Saturday
9:00–5:00. Closed July 4th, Thanksgiving, and
Christmas.*
Admission: Free.
*Guided Tour: Person in charge explains workings of the mill
and its history. Large groups should write well in
advance.*

3. Pierce Mill

This is an authentic restoration of an early grist mill built in Rock Creek Park by Isaac Pierce in 1820. It is the last of eight mills that once were in operation in the park.

Today a working miller with costumed helpers grind wheat into flour.

Check for periodic demonstrations in butter churning and batter-cake making.

Pierce Mill
Rock Creek Park
Tilden Street & Beach Drive, N.W.
Washington, D.C. 20015. Tel. 426-6908

All ages.   Individuals & groups.
Days & Hours: Open daily 9:00–5:00.
Admission: Free.
Guided Tours: Not available.

MUSEUM OF THE AMERICAN REVOLUTION

The Society of the Cincinnati, named after the general whose heroism saved Rome from invaders, was founded in 1783 by American officers of the Continental Army. George Washington served as its first President General until his death in 1799.

The Society's museum, a beautiful townhouse, contains a collection of Revolutionary War relics, including swords, firearms, and uniforms of French regiments and the naval units that participated in the American Revolution.

Anderson House Museum—Society of the Cincinnati
2118 Massachusetts Avenue, N.W.
Washington, D.C. 20008. Tel. 785-2040

Ages 12 and up.   Individuals & groups.
Days & Hours: Tuesday–Saturday 2:00–4:00.
Admission: Free.
Guided Tour: By appointment. Groups should write or tele-
                 phone in advance.

PLANTATIONS

1. Gunston Hall

The builder of this 5,000-acre estate, George Mason, whom Thomas Jefferson called the "wisest man of his generation," was often referred to as the "pen of the Revolution." He was the author of the Virginia Declaration of Rights which became the chief basis for the Federal Bill of Rights and the French Declaration of the Rights of Man.

Perhaps the earliest civil rightist, George Mason refused to sign the Constitution because it did not sufficiently safeguard the rights of the individual or adequately provide for the abolition of slavery.

In addition to the mansion itself, with its impressive interiors, Gunston Hall is famous for its gardens, its 12-foot-high boxwood trees, and the many cultural and entertainment events that take place each year—among them the Fairfax Hunt Meet, Carols by Candlelight, and the Historic Garden Week.

Gunston Hall Plantation (23 miles from D.C.)
Lorton, Va. 22079. Tel. (703) 550-9220

Ages 6 and up.   Individuals & groups.
Days & Hours: Daily 9:00–5:00. Closed Christmas.
Admission: *Children: $.50. Adults: $1.50.*
Guided Tour: *Upon request. Large groups should write or telephone in advance.*

2. Sully Plantation

This 3,111-acre plantation is little changed since it was built in 1794. It is an excellent example of preservation, with its handblown window panes, original fireplace, and hand-forged locks.

It was built by Robert E. Lee's uncle, Richard Bland Lee (one of the founders of Phi Beta Kappa), whose vote in the Congress was a deciding factor in establishing our capital on the shores of the Potomac.

Colonial-costumed hostesses act as guides on tours of the smokehouse, wine cellar, and log schoolhouse.

A highlight is the "Plantation Days" Arts and Crafts Festival in May. Artists and craftsmen demonstrate spinning and weaving, sheep shearing, shoemaking, and candle dipping, among other crafts.

Sully Plantation (25 miles from D.C.)
Box 231
Chantilly, Va. 22021. Tel. (703) 437-1794

All ages.   Individuals & groups.
Days & Hours: *Daily 10:00–5:00. Closed Christmas.*
Admission: *Children under 16: $.25. Adults: $.50.*
Guided Tour: *By appointment. Write or telephone one week in advance.*

3. Woodlawn Plantation

The 2,000-acre Woodlawn Plantation is one of the most historic places in the Washington area.

Originally part of George Washington's Mt. Vernon estate, the plantation's mansion was designed in 1805 by Dr. William Thornton, the first architect of the Capitol Building.

Adults and older children are fascinated by the architecture and the furnishings of the interior. Younger children find the "Touch and Try" exhibit hard to leave. Here they roll hoops, work on looms, practice the fiddle, play games, and clutch a toy or doll of the 1800s.

On special occasions, performances of Revolutionary War music, demonstrations of musketry, and marches by uniformed men help recapture the spirit of our early colorful days.

Woodlawn Plantation (13 miles from D.C.)
9000 Route #1

Alexandria, Va. 22309

Mailing address: Box 37, Mt. Vernon, Va. 22121.

Tel. (703) 780-3118

All ages.   Individuals & groups.
Day's & Hours: Daily 9:30–4:30. Closed Christmas.
Admission: Children: $.60. Adults $1.25. Special rates for all
groups of 15 or more.
Guided Tour: By appointment. Large groups should write or
telephone two weeks in advance.

PORTRAITS OF GREAT AMERICANS

Here's a chance to "meet" the great Americans of our history.

The National Portrait Gallery contains more than 600 portraits of U.S. Presidents, American Indians, generals, explorers, scientists, writers, and actors in marble and bronze and on canvas.

The National Portrait Gallery and the National Collection of Fine Arts share the old Patent Building, one of the oldest structures in Washington and the site of Lincoln's second Inaugural Ball.

• At the Smithsonian National Portrait Gallery.

POST OFFICE

A country-store Post Office that operated in Headsville, West Virginia, from 1861 to 1914 was transplanted to the Smithsonian in 1971, "lock, stock and barrel."

It now functions as a United States Postal Service substation, sells stamps, and forwards mail postmarked "Smithsonian Station."
• At the Smithsonian Museum of History and Technology.

REPORTING THE NEWS

The history of reporting in America, from the 17th century to the present, is on view in the Henry R. Luce Hall of News Reporting. Some of the equipment displayed includes teletype machines, newsreels, and space satellites. A special Apollo II moon camera is in continuous operation.

Exhibits trace the influence of these modern inventions on the way news is presented. There is also a collection of rare newspapers and photographs, and a slide show.
• At the Smithsonian Museum of History and Technology.

RIFLE MUSEUM

Arms and their relation to American history are featured in the National Rifle Museum, founded in 1871. More than 1,000 firearms, including antique and modern shotguns, pistols, and rifles, are displayed in 72 cases.

Foreign arms, including oddities from the Far East, are also exhibited.

National Rifle Association Firearms Museum
1600 Rhode Island Avenue, N.W.
Washington, D.C. 20036. Tel. 783-6505, Ext. 227

All ages.   Individuals & groups up to 30 persons.
Days & Hours: Daily 10:00–4:00. Closed Christmas, New Year's,
and Easter Sunday.
Admission: Free.
Guided Tour: For groups only. Write or telephone one week in
advance.

THE STAR-SPANGLED BANNER
FLAG HOUSE

Contrary to general belief, Betsy Ross had nothing to do with the making of the banner that stirred the Washington lawyer Francis Scott Key to write our National Anthem.

Betsy Ross was a Philadelphia upholsterer and flag-maker who was selected to make the first flag as described by Congress in 1777: "that the flag of the United States be thirteen stripes alternate red and white, that the Union be 13 stars white in a blue field representing a new constellation."

The Star-Spangled Banner Flag House, built in 1793 and restored in 1927, is where Mary Pickersgill sewed the Star-Spangled Banner with its 15 stars and stripes that was raised over Fort McHenry and inspired Francis Scott Key on that morning of September 14, 1814.

The flag itself is on display at the Smithsonian Museum

of History and Technology (its original size, 30 × 42 feet, having been reduced by overly patriotic souvenir collectors), but there are artifacts in the house, including rifles, a snare drum, and a stone map of the United States.

Star-Spangled Banner Flag House (40 miles from D.C.)
844 E. Pratt Street
Baltimore, Md. 21202. Tel. (301) 837-1793

All ages.   Individuals & groups.
Days & Hours: Tuesday–Saturday 10:00–4:00, Sunday 2:00–4:30.
Closed Christmas, New Year's, Easter.
Admission: Children: Free. Adults: $1.
Guided Tour: Groups should write or telephone in advance.

VEHICLES

1. One way to trace America's growth and expansion is to study the way our pioneers moved across the country, transporting families, belongings, and dreams.

An exciting display of vehicles at the Museum of History and Technology includes horse-drawn and motor-driven conveyances, the famous "one-hoss shay," and early fire engines. A collection of early automobiles contains the first Duryea (1893), the Haynes (1894), a 1903 Oldsmobile, a 1913 Ford Model T, and other mobile treasures, among them a ten-speed bicycle.

• At the Smithsonian Museum of History and Technology.

2. The National Capital Trolley Museum appeals to all ages and serves as a fascinating introduction to this type of vehicle.

The collection of American and European trolleys includes a Sweeper 07 built in 1889 and used until 1962 to maintain the Washington area trolley system during snowy weather. There is also an American deck-roof trolley of 1918, as well as vehicles from Vienna and Graz, built in the early 1900s.

Special trolley events, usually on the third Sunday of the month, take place at the museum. These are listed in the local newspapers or are announced over the radio.

A thrilling experience is the ride on the historic street-car through the rolling hills of Maryland.

National Capital Trolley Museum (16 miles from D.C.)
Bonifant Road between Layhill Road &
    New Hampshire Ave.
Wheaton, Maryland 20902
Mailing Address: P. O. Box 5795, Bethesda, Md. 20014.
    Tel. (301) 384-9797

All ages.   Individuals & groups.
Days & Hours: *Open during the summer through Labor Day on Wednesdays, Thursdays, and Fridays 12:00–4:00. Weekends all year 12:00–5:00. Closed Christmas and New Year's.*
Admission: *Free. Trolley rides are $.25 for children under 18 and $.50 for adults. Infants under 2 free.*
Guided Tour: *Not available. School groups should telephone (301) 585-7062 in advance.*

4 Animals, Gardens, and Nature

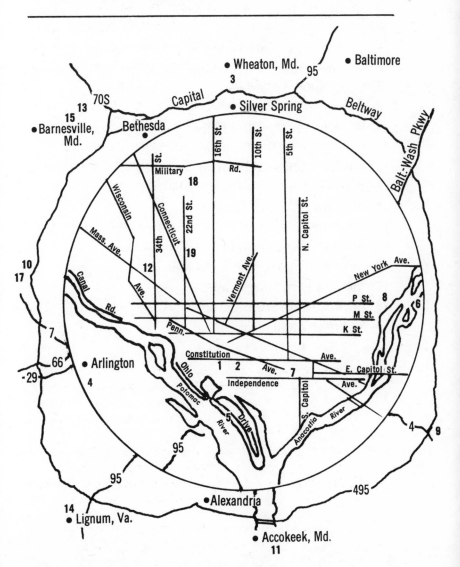

MAP LEGEND

1. Smithsonian Museum of History and Technology
2. Smithsonian Museum of Natural History
3. Brookside Nature Center & Gardens
4. Animal Welfare League
5. United States Park Police
6. Kenilworth Aquatic Gardens
7. U. S. Botanic Garden
8. National Arboretum
9. Blackwater Wildlife Refuge
10. Great Falls of the Potomac
11. National Colonial Farm
12. Washington Cathedral
13. Al-Marah Arabian Horse Farm
14. Rapidan River Farm
15. Arabian Horse Museum
16. American Work Horse Museum
17. Morven Park Equestrian Institute
18. Rock Creek Nature Center
19. National Zoological Park

BEEHIVE

A beehive with 60,000 inhabitants is on exhibit in season behind the Farm Machinery Hall in the Museum of History and Technology.
• At the Smithsonian Museum of History and Technology.

See *Brookside Nature Center* (below) and *Rock Creek Nature Center* (page 80) for other beehives.

BIRDS OF THE WORLD

Bird-lovers will appreciate this display of feathered creatures, from all parts of the world, in realistic settings.

Among the skillfully-executed exhibits are birds in flight and special-interest birds such as the Antarctic penguin, the pheasant with its enormous, colored plumes, and the ostrich, complete with just-hatched babies.

Other displays illustrate the migration, reproduction, and feeding habits of birds.

Be sure to look at the fascinating exhibit of birds of all shapes, sizes, and colors.
• At the Smithsonian Museum of Natural History.

Also see Birdhouse, under *Zoo,* in this chapter (page 81).

BROOKSIDE NATURE CENTER

Exhibits at Brookside Nature Center focus on the natural history of the Metropolitan Washington area.

Attractions include aquariums, an indoor turtle pool, a live beehive, slide shows, and movies.

Brookside Nature Center (6 miles from D.C.)
1400 Glenallan Avenue
Wheaton, Md. 20902. Tel. (301) 946-9071

All ages.   Individuals & groups.
Days & Hours: *Tuesday–Saturday 9:00–5:00. Sunday: 1:00–5:00.*
             Closed holidays.
Admission: *Free.*
Guided Tour: *By appointment. Telephone one to two months*
             in advance.

CATS AND DOGS

For children who like cats or dogs or both, the Washington area has special attractions, and we are listing two.

1. The Animal Welfare League of Arlington welcomes children to visit its shelter to listen to a talk on animal care and on animal welfare laws.

Animal Welfare League (1 mile from D.C.)
2800 South Taylor Street
Arlington, Va. 22206. Tel. (703) 931-9241

Ages 5 and up.   Individuals & groups.
Days & Hours: *By appointment.*
Admission: *Free.*
Guided Tour: *Write or telephone at least one week in ad-*
             vance.

2. Police Dog Show: The U.S. Park Police puts on shows by their highly-trained Police dogs for local groups of children.

The dogs demonstrate how they overcome obstacles, climb ladders, scale walls, go through hoops, and obey voice commands.

United States Park Police
1100 Ohio Drive, S.W.
Washington, D.C. 20242. Tel. 426-6831

All ages.   Individuals & groups.
Days & Hours: *1st and 3rd Tuesday of the month, September– May.*
Admission: *Free.*
Guided Tour: *Not available. For dog demonstrations, write to Chief, U.S. Park Police, at the above address. State number in your group and dates you would prefer to see the performance.*

DINOSAURS

Let your imagination run wild as you gaze on the reconstructed dinosaur bones. Picture this huge creature walking the earth!

There are also other prehistoric specimens around you. Here is one, 125 feet long from its tiny head to its lashing tail.

Scale dioramas show animals in their habitat, and flying reptile reconstructions hang on the nearby walls.

Look at them from all angles.
• At the Smithsonian Museum of Natural History.

ELEPHANT

The largest African bush elephant ever shot stands three stories high in the Museum of Natural History. He looks unbelievable, exciting, frightening.

This magnificent beast, more than 13 feet tall and weighing 12 tons when captured, was first sighted in Angola by J. J. Fénykövi, a Hungarian-born engineer. Following the 24-inch tracks he noticed in the bush led to Fénykövi's finding and subsequent shooting of the elephant.

• At the Smithsonian Museum of Natural History.

FARMS

Close to thirty Maryland farms open their gates to visitors the last Sunday in June. "Welcome Farm" is the name of the event.

So, if you want to see how tobacco leaves grow, how holly trees look in summer, or how farm animals spend a Sunday in June, write to the University of Maryland's School of Agriculture, College Park, Maryland, 20742 and ask for the "Welcome Farm" list.

FOSSILS

Even if you're not a fossil fancier, it should be interesting to meet a creature that lived 1.6 billion years ago.

At the Hall of Fossils, Plants, and Invertebrate Animals, you can meet the Grinflint chert, the oldest known fossil on record, found in northern Ontario.

The exhibits explain fossils and also the methods by which their age is determined.

• At the Smithsonian Museum of Natural History.

FOX HUNTING

Fox hunting—the sport of chasing a fox with horses and hounds—was brought to America from England, where it was established in the early 18th century. It became popular in Maryland and Virginia, and is still conducted every year from the fall to the spring.

Here are two hunts that visitors might like to attend.

The Loudon Hunt (40 miles from D.C.)
Oatlands Estate
Leesburg, Virginia
Tel. (703) 777-1030 or (703) 338-4265

The Thanksgiving Hunt Week at Charlottesville, Virginia, begins with the Blessing of the Hounds at Grace Church on Thanksgiving Day. For more information write:

Charlottesville and Albemarle County Chamber
    of Commerce
P.O. Box 1564
Charlottesville, Virginia, 22902

FRUIT, BERRY, AND VEGETABLE PICKING

Pick your own ripened berries, fruits, and pumpkins in nearby Maryland and Virginia. For specific information and locations, consult local newspapers or write to:

1. Department of Agriculture and Resource Economics
   University of Maryland
   College Park, Maryland 20742

2. Fruit Marketing Agent
   Virginia Department of Agriculture
   203 N. Governor Street
   Richmond, Va. 23219

GARDENS

1. Brookside Gardens

This 25-acre garden has a conservatory greenhouse filled with plants and flowers, many of them exotic and from far-away lands.

See the growing coffee tree; its branches laden with bananas and chrysanthemums are trained into flowing cascades. There is the annual Christmas flower show with its traditional seasonal plants such as the Jerusalem cherry, cyclamen, and kalanchoe. The spring flower show ushers in displays of Easter lilies, azaleas, hydrangeas, fuchsia, and dogwood.

A talk on the growth and care of plants and flowers is available on request.

> Brookside Gardens (10 miles from D.C.)
> 1500 Glenallan Avenue
> Wheaton, Md. 20902. Tel. (301) 949-8230
>
> All ages.   Individuals & groups.
> *Days & Hours: Open all year, Tuesday–Saturday 9:00–5:00. Sunday 1:00–6:00. Closed Christmas.*
> *Admission: Free.*
> *Guided Tour: Lasts about 45 minutes. Inquire about schedule.*

2. Kenilworth Aquatic Gardens

These eleven acres of ponds can aptly be called a water garden. Some of the water lilies are six feet in diameter and can easily hold a 90-pound child.

Among its rare plants are the Victoria cruziane, the huge-leaved specimen that comes from the Amazon basin; and the Egyptian lotus, reputed to be Cleopatra's favorite.

Try to catch the "night-blooming" water lilies before they close up for the day. Get there before midday during their blooming season. In mid-June you may see 70 varieties of day-blooming water lilies; in the latter part of July or early August the day-and-night-blooming tropical water lilies burst into flower.

Inquire about the special environmental education programs.

> Kenilworth Aquatic Gardens
> Anacostia Avenue at Douglas Street, N.E.

Washington, D.C. 20019. Tel. 426-6905

All ages.   Individuals & groups.
Days & Hours: *Daily 7:30 A.M. to sundown.*
Admission: *Free.*
Guided Tour: *June through August. For groups only, but indi-
viduals may join scheduled tour. Telephone
426-6917, or write Superintendent, National Cap-
ital Parks-East, 5210 Indian Head Highway, Oxon
Hill, Md. 20021, two weeks in advance.*

3. U.S. Botanic Garden

No matter what time of year, a visit to the U.S. Botanic
Garden is a breathtaking experience.

It is a storehouse of plants and flowers from the
Americas and around the world. Its spacious Conservatory
grows more than 8,000 species and varieties of plants,
including the bunyabunya tree of Australia, the lychee
and nut tree from China, the tapioca from Brazil, and the
Arabian coffee tree.

Other exotic flowers and fruits include 90 varieties of
azaleas and an extensive orchid collection. The Botanic
Garden is also famous for its flower shows. The Annual
Easter Show, with its thousands of spring plants, and the
Chrysanthemum, Poinsettia, and Christmas Green shows
are attended by thousands each year.

A favorite feature of the Spring Flower Festival is the
demonstration of the Japanese flower arrangement
known as "ikebana" with its traditional Tea Ceremony.

U.S. Botanic Garden
Maryland Avenue, near First Street, S.W.
Washington, D.C. 20024. Tel. 225-8333

All ages.   Individuals & groups.

Days & Hours: *Daily from 9:00–4:00. Closed Christmas and New Year's.*

Admission: *Free.*

Guided Tour: *For groups only. Write or telephone far in advance.*

4. U.S. National Arboretum

The U.S. National Arboretum was established in 1927 by Act of Congress to cultivate trees, plants, shrubs, and flowers; to conduct research on plant life; and to educate the public in these areas.

This 415-acre arboretum features Oriental plants, dogwoods, azaleas, the magnificent Fern Valley, the Youth Gardens for local children, the Braille Trail for the blind, and the Cryptomeria Valley of the Garden Clubs of America, filled with unusual plants.

Inquire about the data sheet that gives the approximate time that the various trees and plants bloom.

U.S. National Arboretum
24th & R Streets, N.E.
Washington, D.C. 20002. Tel. 399-5400, Ext. 71/72 or
   396-0030

All ages.   Individuals & groups.

Days & Hours: *Open all year except Christmas. Summer: weekdays 8:00–7:00; weekends 10:00–7:00. Winter: weekdays 8:00–5:00; weekends 10:00–5:00.*

Admission: *Free.*

Guided Tour: *For groups of 10 or more, write or telephone three weeks in advance.*

GEESE, DUCKS, BALD EAGLES

75,000 to 100,000 Canadian geese flying south make a stopover each year at the 11,216-acre Blackwater National Wildlife Refuge. These geese and as many as 125,000 ducks assemble here in season. No one knows why.

The arrival season begins late September or early October and reaches its peak in late November when the geese begin to fly to a warmer climate. Around 30,000 of these birds remain here all winter.

Originally a shelter for ducks, the Refuge is now home for an assortment of other birds, waterfowl, and small animals. Some endangered species, including our national symbol, the bald eagle, found only in North America, are protected here.

Dark brown with light markings at birth, the bald eagle's colors change with age, and his white-feathered head gives the appearance of baldness.

Most of the species have been killed, and the remaining, numbering about 15,000, have been protected by Federal law since 1940.

The Refuge is a distance from Washington, but nowhere else can one see such a spectacle. Warning: Stay away from June through August when the insects are at their biting best.

Blackwater Wildlife Refuge (90 miles from D.C.)
Route 1, Box 121
Cambridge, Md. 21613. Tel. (301) 228-2677

All ages.   Individuals & groups.

Days & Hours: *Daily until sunset. Closed Christmas.*
Admission: *Free.*
Guided Tour: *Not available.*

GREAT FALLS OF THE POTOMAC

The Great Falls of the Potomac is the most spectacular scenic attraction in the Washington area. At times more water tumbles over its 50-foot drop than over the falls at Niagara, New York.

There is a Visitors Center and a small museum with special programs featuring the area.

Great Falls of the Potomac (9 miles from D.C.)
9200 Old Dominion Drive
Great Falls, Va. 22066. Tel. 759-2915

The falls of course can be seen at all times, but for special programs and a guided tour telephone in advance.

HERB GARDENS

1. The National Colonial Farm at Accokeek, Maryland, cultivates a kitchen and medicinal herb garden.

National Colonial Farm (20 miles from D.C.)
Route 1, Box 697
Accokeek, Md. 20607. Tel. (301) 283-2113

Ages 11 and up.   Individuals & groups.
Days & Hours: *Daily June 1–Labor Day 10:00–5:00. Other times by appointment.*

Admission:　　Children: $.25. Adults: $.50.
Guided Tour:　For groups only. Telephone in advance.

2. The Washington Cathedral grows a great variety of herbs, with an herb cottage nearby where visitors may purchase them freshly grown, for flavor or scent.

Washington Cathedral
Massachusetts & Wisconsin Avenues, N.W.
Washington, D.C. 20016. Tel. 966-3500, Ext. 249

All ages.　Individuals & groups.
Days & Hours: Daily 9:00–5:00.
Admission:　　Free.
Guided Tour:　Throughout the day. Only groups need write or
　　　　　　　telephone one month in advance for reserva-
　　　　　　　tions.

HORSES

1. Arabian Horse Farm

Reputed to be the largest and finest of its kind in the world, the Al-Marah Arabian Horse Farm is located on 2,800 acres of Maryland's rolling pastureland.

Children like to watch the horses and will want to admire the foals or colts that can be viewed from January through July. The Trophy Room is of great interest to young and old.

The barns and rings where the horses are trained and where they perform on special occasions are open to visitors.

Four times a year, "Club Days" with special demonstrations are featured. For a "Club Days" schedule, ask to be put on their mailing list.

Al-Marah Arabian Horse Farm (35 miles from D.C.)
Box 401, Peachtree Road
Barnesville, Md. 20703. Tel. (301) 948-5013

All ages. Individuals & groups.
Days & Hours: Daily 9:00–4:00. Closed Thanksgiving and
            Christmas.
Admission: Free.
Guided Tour: For groups only, but individuals may join sched-
            uled tour. Write or telephone two weeks in
            advance.

2. Morgan Horse Farm
Visitors to the Rapidan River Farm can meet the famous Morgan horse. He's America's Cavalry favorite—outstanding for his strength and endurance, in which he surpasses the Arabian stallion.

Harness horses are also trained here, and films and lectures are available for large groups.

Rapidan River Farm (60 miles from D.C.)
Box 45
Lignum, Va. 22726. Tel. (703) 825-8326

All ages. Individuals & groups.
Days & Hours: Monday–Saturday 10:00–4:00. Closed Christmas.
Admission: Free.
Guided Tour: By appointment. Large groups should write or
            telephone one week in advance.

3. Horse Museums

The only Arabian horse museum in the world was established here to preserve art, literature, and historic films that record the heritage and magnificence of this breed.

The museum provides information on the horse's care and management. It contains a library with books dating back to 1580, and a Hall of Fame to which noted Arabian horses are nominated.

> Arabian Horse Museum (35 miles from D.C.)
> Box 303
> Barnesville, Md. 20703. Tel. (301) 972-0568
>
> Ages 9 and up. Individuals & groups.
> *Days & Hours: Open daily during summer, weekends during spring and fall. Check dates.*
> *Admission:*   *Free.*
> *Guided Tour: By appointment. Groups may also visit during winter. Write or telephone at least one week in advance.*

The American Work Horse Museum was established to honor the work horse, and to pay tribute to his 200-year role in the growth and development of our country.

The museum contains thousands of articles of horse equipment and implements, including blacksmith riggings and veterinary supplies.

> American Work Horse Museum
>   (39 miles from D.C.)
> Paeonian Springs, Va. 22129. Tel. (703) 338-6920

Ages 8 and up.   Individuals & groups.
Days & Hours: By appointment. Closed during the winter.
Admission: Free.
Guided Tour: Write or telephone in advance.

4. School for Riders

The aim of the Morven Park International Equestrian Institute is "to teach people to teach riding, after they've been taught themselves."

The school houses eighty of the best Thoroughbreds in the country, including old Olympic performers that have been donated by their owners.

Classes are usually held weekdays in the mornings, and students often practice jumping or lunging over fences on Thursday and Friday afternoons.

There are no guided tours, but visitors are welcome to observe classes in progress and attend the weekend in May when a three-phase event is held, as well as the graduation weekend.

Be sure to tour the Morven Estate when you visit the school, and see its formal gardens and the mansion with furnishings from three continents.

Morven Park Equestrian Institute (45 miles from D.C.)
Route 2, Box 8
Leesburg, Va. 22075. Tel. (703) 777-2890

All ages.   Groups only.
Days & Hours: By appointment.
Admission: Free.
Guided Tour: No scheduled tour, but arrangements may be made for group visits. Write or telephone in advance.

ROCK CREEK NATURE CENTER

Rock Creek Nature Center is a park complex of buildings and nature trails designed to teach youngsters about our natural world and man's relationship to it.

An exhibit hall displays examples of local animal life, including a live bee colony, and minerals. The nature walks led by park rangers and scientists usually emphasize a single theme (such as ecology, mushrooms, Indian life) and are given weekdays to accommodate school groups. Weekend tours are also available.

The Rock Creek Planetarium is part of the Nature Center. See "Stars," Chapter 9.

Rock Creek Nature Center
Military & Glover Roads, N.W.
Washington, D.C. 20015. Tel. 426-6892

All ages.   Individuals & groups.
Days & Hours: Monday–Saturday 9:30–5:00. Sunday 12:00–6:00. Closed holidays.
Admission: Free.
Guided Tour: For specific information about programs and activities write Superintendent, National Capital Parks-West, 1100 Ohio Drive S.W., Washington, D.C. 20242. Large groups, classes, or Scout troops should telephone in advance.

TIGER

This Bengal tiger, believed to be the largest ever caught, is a native of northern India, and measures 11 feet 1 inch in length and weighs 857 pounds.

Presented to the Smithsonian in 1969, this mounted tiger is an example of a now-vanishing species.

• At the Smithsonian Museum of Natural History.

ZOO

The United States Zoological Park is one of our national treasures. It contains thousands of animals, birds, reptiles, and many rare species, some of them gifts from foreign governments to our country. A large number of animals are threatened with extinction. Among them, all to be found at the zoo, are the:

American alligator	Lion-tailed macaque
Galapagos tortoise	Orangutan
Golden marmoset	Parma wallaby
Great Indian rhino	Polar bear
Grizzly bear	Pygmy hippopotamus
Hawaiian goose	Syrian brown bear

The zoo also maintains a large research center to study animal life and to help preserve the various species seriously threatened with extinction.

Listed here are only a few of the exhibits that are especially popular with children. We suggest that youngsters go "zoo" for themselves.

National Zoological Park
Washington, D.C. 20008. Tel. 628-4422

Entrance at Connecticut Avenue, N.W., 3000 block.

All ages.   Individuals & groups.
Days & Hours: Gates open daily at 6:00 A.M. Buildings open
9:00–4:30 in winter, 9:00–6:00 in summer.
Admission: Free.
Guided Tour: Volunteers of the Friends of the Zoo conduct
tours from mid-March to May. Reservations must
be made one month in advance. Call 232-7703.
Between April and the end of October the zoo operates a train
that takes visitors to the Bird House, the Elephant House, and the
Cafeteria for a nominal fee. Hold on to your ticket and reboard
the train as often as you wish, at no extra charge.

Bird House

The Bird House has a free-flight room equipped with special temperature and humidity controls for its large collection of tropical birds. Among its thriving inhabitants are hoopoes, fairy bluebirds, cock-of-the-rocks, and Rothschild's starlings.

Great Flight Cage

The Great Flight Cage, next to the bird house, is a circular cage, 130 feet in diameter, with a 90-foot-high center mast. The entire cage is covered with a vinyl-coated fine wire mesh.

While the birds fly freely among them, visitors who enter the cage through a set of glass doors walk leisurely amid boulders, pools, and waterfalls.

Laughing Jackass

The zoo has a jackass from Australia which their natives call the "kookaburra." The out-of-this-world sound he makes well earns him the name he bears.

Outer Space Chimpanzee

Ham, the chimpanzee that made a sixteen-minute trip in an outer space capsule in 1961, is a permanent resident in the zoo.

Pandas

A gift from the People's Republic of China to the people of the United States, the two black-and-white bearlike cousins of the raccoon family arrived in Washington in April 1972.

As many as 75,000 visitors in a single day have come to watch the clowning Ling-Ling take a bath in her wooden tub or nibble on her favorite carrot. Hsing-Hsing, the male member of the team, is serious, reserved, and antisocial. Let the world watch fur-brained Ling-Ling doing her antics, Hsing-Hsing cares not. He is content to spend most of his time in his air-conditioned apartment wondering about the funny people looking his way.

Smokey the Bear

Smokey, the symbol of "Only You Can Prevent Forest Fires," was known everywhere for his interest in preserving wildlife and discouraging forest fires. Before his death, he was a member of the zoo family.

White Tigress

The rare Mohini Rewa or Enchantress of Rewa is the only animal of its kind in the United States.

A native of the small province of Rewa, India, this blue-eyed tigress with a coat striped from light cream to black was raised by the maharaja of the province.

5 On the Job

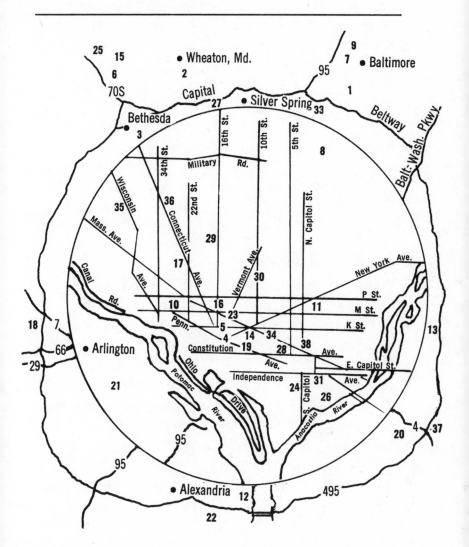

MAP LEGEND

1. Agricultural Research Center
2. Bagelmasters, Inc.
3. Metropolitan Academy of Ballet
4. American Security & Trust Co.
5. National Savings & Trust Co.
6. Vie de France Corp.
7. Carling Brewing Co.
8. Flame of Hope Candle Factory
9. Goetze's Candy Co.
10. Craftsmen of Chelsea Court
11. D. C. Farmers Market
12. Copeland Flag Co.
13. Briggs & Co.
14. Washington Gas Light Co.
15. Hines Hatchery
16. Executive House
17. Sheraton-Park Hotel
18. National Fruit Product Co.
19. Al's Magic Shop
20. U.S. Defense Mapping Agency Topographic Center
21. Maryland & Virginia Milk Producers Association
22. *Alexandria Gazette*
23. *Washington Post*
24. *Washington Star*
25. *The Sentinel*
26. U.S. Naval Photographic Center
27. Schaeffer's Piano Co.
28. Metropolitan Police Department
29. Colortone Press
30. Merkle Press
31. Capitol Page School
32. Herman Perlman Sculptures
33. Divers World Skin Diving School
34. Chesapeake & Potomac Telephone Co.
35. WTTG-TV
36. WMAL-TV
37. Tobacco Experimental Farm
38. Washington City Post Office

AGRICULTURAL RESEARCH

The Beltsville Agricultural Research Center is part of the United States Department of Agriculture. Half of the two thousand employees here are scientists studying and doing experiments in agriculture and related fields. Their findings not only benefit our own people, but peoples around the world.

Over 1,000 buildings (laboratories, greenhouses, and barns) house more than 10,000 cattle, hogs, sheep, chickens, and small research animals.

The tour varies with age and interest level of each group. Usually, animal and plant-science research projects are visited; a slide show explaining the work at the Center is available on request.

Bring your camera, and don't forget raincoat and rubbers if it looks threatening. Tours go on, rain or shine. For groups larger than fifteen persons it is advisable to charter a bus to get the maximum benefit of the guided tour.

Agricultural Research Center (15 miles from D.C.) Beltsville, Md. 20705. Tel. (301) 344-2483

Ages 10 and up.   Groups only.
Days & Hours: *By appointment.*
Admission: *Free.*
Guided Tour: *Lasts about two hours. Write or telephone in advance.*

BAGEL

Although opinions may differ whether a bagel is a round piece of dough with a hole in the center or a hole with dough around it, a visit to Bagelmasters will show you every step that goes into the making of this baked delicacy.

Bagelmasters, Inc. (15 miles from D.C.)
2421 Reedie Drive
Wheaton, Md. 20902. Tel. (301) 933-0200

All ages.   Groups only.
Days & Hours: By appointment.
Admission: Free.
Guided Tour: Telephone two weeks in advance.

BALLET LESSONS

Ballet-interested young people between the ages of eight and sixteen are welcome to observe classes in session at the Metropolitan Academy of Ballet. (Also see the entry "Backstage at the Ballet," in chapter eight.)

Metropolitan Academy of Ballet (5 miles from D.C.)
4836 Rugby Avenue
Bethesda, Md. 20014. Tel. (301) 654-2233

Ages 8–16.   Individuals or small groups.
*Days & Hours: Monday–Friday 1:00–6:30, Saturday 9:30–12:30.
           Closed holidays, and from August 1st to Sep-
           tember 15.*

Admission: Free.
Guided Tour: Not available. To observe a class write or call Charles Dickson, director, one week in advance.

BANKS

A bank is an institution that affects the lives of every one of us. When you take this behind-the-scenes tour, you will get an inside look at all phases of banking operations, from the opening of an account to a trip to the vault.

1. American Security & Trust Company
   15th Street and Pennsylvania Avenue, N.W.
   Washington, D.C. 20013. Tel. 624-4225

   Ages 12 and up. Groups only.
   Days & Hours: By appointment.
   Admission: Free.
   Guided Tour: Write or telephone William Hubbell's (V.P.) office, two weeks in advance.

2. National Savings & Trust Company
   15th Street at New York Avenue, N.W.
   Washington, D.C. 20005. Tel. 659-5900

   Ages 10 and up. Groups only but individuals may join scheduled tour.
   Days & Hours: By appointment.
   Admission: Free.
   Guided Tour: Write or telephone Helen Coll (Senior V.P.) one week in advance.

BREAD

No need to visit France for the best French bread around. You can get it right in Washington.

A special brick and stainless-steel oven imported from France, complete with a French baker, produces more than 15,000 loaves daily in Rockville, Maryland, just outside Washington.

Tours include an explanation of the equipment and the ingredients. Following a question-and-answer period, each visitor is given a loaf of freshly-baked Vie de France bread to take home.

Vie de France Corporation (7 miles from D.C.)
12130 Nebel Street
Rockville, Md. 20852. Tel. (301) 770-3575

All ages.   Groups only.
Days & Hours: By appointment.
Admission: Free.
Guided Tour: Telephone Arthur J. Stouffs, Manager, one
                         month in advance.

BREWERY

A visit to the Carling Brewery offers secrets no can of beer will ever reveal. For example, do you know that the best hops used in beer-making grow on tall vines in the Pacific Northwest, or that corn and rice help give beer its pale color and improve its shelf-life?

At the Carling plant you'll see how ingredients are crushed, boiled, cooled, strained, and aged to produce ale and beer. You'll also enjoy seeing how 1,000 cans are filled and sealed every minute by the automatic packaging machine.

Carling Brewing Company (40 miles from D.C.)
4501 Hollins Ferry Road
Baltimore, Md. 21227. Tel. (301) 242-5500, Ext. 238

Ages 7 and up.   Individuals & groups.
Days & Hours: *See below.*
Admission: *Free.*
Guided Tour: *Tours for the general public, lasting about 35 minutes, are held on Tuesdays at 10:00 and Thursdays at 2:00. No reservations are necessary, but groups of more than 20 persons should telephone at least two weeks in advance, and arrangements will be made for other days if more convenient.*

CANDLEMAKING

You'll enjoy the magic of candlemaking at this center where the wax is melted, colored, perfumed, and poured into molds for the handsome Flame of Hope Candles.

What makes it unusual is that the workers are all retarded men and women. The project was originally started by the Kennedy family, and today these handmade candles are sold in stores throughout the country.

Occupational Training Center
Flame of Hope Candle Factory
405 Riggs Road, N.E.
Washington, D.C. 20011. Tel. 529-0070

Ages 5 and up.   Groups up to 20 persons. Individuals may join
                 scheduled tour.
Days & Hours: *By appointment.*
Admission: *Free.*
Guided Tour: *By appointment. Telephone Martin Weiss,
                 Workshop Director.*

CANDY

A tour of Goetze's Candy Company is a mouth-watering experience.

Goetze's began in 1895 in a small home basement; now it occupies a spacious modern plant where forty-five tons of caramel candy are produced daily.

High-speed automatic equipment, controlled by computers, performs all the steps of candy-making, from the milling of sugar to the packaging of the finished nuggets. The tour shows each step.

Goetze's Candy Co., Inc. (40 miles from D.C.)
3900 E. Monument Street
Baltimore, Md. 21205. Tel. (301) 342-2010

Ages 7 and up.   Groups only.
Days & Hours: *By appointment. Closed to visitors from October
                 to May.*
Admission: *Free.*
Guided Tour: *Tuesdays and Thursdays at 9:30 A.M. Write or
                 telephone in advance.*

CRAFTSMEN OF CHELSEA COURT

A group of professional artists called "The Craftsmen of Chelsea Court" create, by hand, unique designs in pottery, silver, enamel, and in stained glass.

See them at work and their finished designs on display.

Craftsmen of Chelsea Court
2909 M Street, N.W.
Washington, D.C. 20007. Tel. 338-4588

Ages 5 and up.   Individuals & groups.
Days & Hours: Tuesday–Saturday 10:00–6:00. Open holidays
except Christmas.
Admission: Free.
Guided Tour:·   By appointment. Write or telephone Ms. Maxine
G. Brown, President.

FAIRS, FEASTS, FESTIVALS, AND MARKETS

The D.C. Farmers Market—located in a 30,000-foot building, air-conditioned in the summer and heated in winter—offers a vast variety of produce directly from the farmer's bushel, ready for the customer's shopping cart.

Washington also has a number of outdoor markets and periodic fairs and festivals, usually from early spring through fall. Nearby Maryland and Virginia communities hold street fairs and festivals and have regularly scheduled market days. A popular one is the Amish Market at Charlotte's Hall, Maryland.

Watch the newspapers or call local Maryland and Virginia tourist bureaus for schedules and exact addresses.

D.C. Farmers Market
1390 Fifth Street, N.E.
Washington, D.C. 20002. Tel. 547-3142

Days & Hours: *Monday–Friday   8:00–6:00.   Saturday–Sunday 8:00–8:00. Closed Christmas.*
Admission: *Free.*
Guided Tour *By appointment. Lasts around one hour. Call George Stevenson, Manager, to make arrangements.*

FIREFIGHTING

Any Fire Department station may be visited by groups of children five years and older.

Of special interest are:

1. The D.C. Fire Station at 1018 13th Street, N.W., with its 85-foot aerial platform truck.

2. The Fire Station at 450 Sixth Street, S.W., with its aerial ladder truck and its Foam and Dry Chemical Unit used to smother fires.

3. The Communications Division, 300 McMillan Drive, N.W., the main receiving and dispatching center for all Fire Department emergency calls in the district.

There is no firefighting museum in the District of Columbia, but plans are underway to erect a National Fire

Museum at 3212 M Street, N.W. For information, call 337-2202.

Of special interest is the 81-foot-long fireboat used by the District of Columbia Fire Department along the shore of the Potomac. The modern fireboat is equipped with apparatus of the latest design and with high-capacity water pumps.

A tour here varies with the age and interest level of the group and may include a demonstration of the boat's equipment, a film, and a question-and-answer period. Be sure to make arrangements in advance.

Also of interest is the Fire Training Academy at 4600 Overlook Avenue, S.W., where members of the District of Columbia Fire Department and other firefighting units, including the Federal and military departments, are trained. Visitors are given explanations and demonstrations of the various equipment used in fire extinguishing.

To arrange visits to the fire stations, the fireboat, and the Fire Training Academy, call the Deputy Fire Chief of the Fire Fighting Division (629-2003) weekdays between 10:00 and 4:00.

FLAG MAKERS

The "Mount Vernon Flag Makers," as the Copeland Company calls itself, create flags for United States Government agencies and foreign embassies.

A visit to this shop usually includes a demonstration of how a flag is made—from the measuring and cutting of the fabric to its completion. On display are flags of nations from around the world.

If time permits, a talk is presented on the history of the flag, followed by a question-and-answer period. Slides with scripts are available on loan to groups.

> The Copeland Company
> 512 N. Pitt Street
> Alexandria, Va. 22314. Tel. 549-1625
>
> Ages 12 and up.   Groups of 10–12 persons.
> *Days & Hours:* *By appointment.*
> *Admission:*   *Free.*
> *Guided Tour:*   *Telephone in advance.*

FRANKFURTERS

In spite of its German origin, the frankfurter is considered as American as apple pie, and is loved by everyone.

At Briggs & Company you can watch all the steps that go into the making of a frankfurter, from the preparation of the meat until it is ready to be eaten.

The tour includes a visit to other meat processing departments as well.

> Briggs & Company (3 miles from D.C.)
> 6601 Columbia Park Road
> Landover, Md. 20785. Tel. (301) 772-7000

Ages 12 and up.   Groups only. 15–40 persons.
Days & Hours: By appointment.
Admission: Free.
Guided Tour: Write or telephone three weeks in advance.

GAS

Natural gas is formed by the continual pressure of rocks, mud, sand, and heat on the remains of animal and plant life of millions of years ago.

The Chinese trapped and sent this fluid through bamboo pipelines some 2,000 years ago; and in Fredonia, New York, the birthplace of natural gas in the United States, a gunsmith, William A. Hart, first made use of it when he found it escaping from the earth.

A tour of the Washington Gas Light Company includes exhibits and movies, and a talk explains how gas is recovered from the earth and tells of its many uses in our daily life.

Washington Gas Light Company
1100 H Street, N.W.
Washington, D.C. 20005. Tel. 624-6209

All ages.   Individuals & groups.
Days & Hours: By appointment.
Admission: Free.
Guided Tour: For local groups. Write or telephone one week in advance.

HATCHERY AND EGGERY

See baby chicks hatching in glass incubators. Watch day-old chicks and various breeds of geese and peafowl.

Eggs are also graded and candled here, and the hatchery has a collection of eggs that range from very small to ostrich-size.

Hines Hatchery (15 miles from D.C.)
17336 George Avenue
Olney, Md. 20832. Tel. (301) 924-3766

All ages.   Groups only, but individuals may join scheduled tours.
Days & Hours: March through May. Monday and Tuesday only.
Admission: Children: $.25.   Adults: $1.25.
Guided Tour: Monday and Tuesday mornings. Telephone in advance.

HOTEL TOURS

1. A tour of the Executive House will take you from the front desk to guest rooms, kitchen, restaurant, and the accounting and sales offices.

Executive House
1515 Rhode Island Avenue, N.W.
Washington, D.C. 20005. Tel. 232-7000

Ages 8 and up.   Groups only.
Days & Hours: By appointment.
Admission: Free.
Guided Tour: Write or telephone in advance, Brian G. Kirby, General Manager.

2. A guided Sheraton-Park Hotel tour includes a visit to the kitchen where the chef will create visual delights out of dough; a tour of the engineering and upholstery departments; and a visit to the key-making section.

Sheraton-Park Hotel
2660 Woodley Road, N.W.
Washington, D.C. 20008. Tel. 265-2000

Ages 8 and up.   Groups only.
Days & Hours: *By appointment.*
Admission: *Free.*
Guided Tour: *Write, or telephone 265-2000, Ext. 2013/4.*

JUICES AND SAUCES

The National Fruit Product Company conducts tours showing how fruits are automatically peeled, juices squeezed, and sauces and vinegars produced.

Of special interest is the apple cider press.

National Fruit Product Company, Inc. (65 miles from
   D.C.)
550 Fairmont Avenue
Winchester, Va. 22601. Tel. (703) 662-3401

Ages 6 and up.   Individuals & groups.
Days & Hours: *By appointment.*
Admission: *Free.*
Guided Tour: *Write two weeks in advance. No tours between*
                 May 1 and September 15.

MAGIC

A visit to Al's Magic Shop will convince you there is no need for secret forces or supernatural powers to perform magic tricks. Anyone with a little practice can make four baby rabbits appear and a whole fan of playing cards disappear.

Al, the magic man, loves to demonstrate his many tricks and help anyone interested in learning what the French call "legerdemain," or just plain old-fashioned sleight of hand tricks.

Fun for children of all ages, from one to one hundred.

Al's Magic Shop
1205 Pennsylvania Avenue, N.W.
Washington, D.C. 20004. Tel. 638-4241

All ages.   Individuals & groups.
Days & Hours: Monday–Saturday 9:00–5:30.
Admission: Free.
Guided Tour: Not available but magic demonstrations are.

MAP MAKING

The techniques of map making will be explained to students of senior high school age and above during a visit to the U.S. Topographic Center of the Defense Mapping Agency.

Students get on-the-spot briefings of the equipment used in map making.

U.S. Defense Mapping Agency Topographic Center
6500 Brooks Lane
Washington, D.C. 20315. Tel. 227-2023/4/5

Ages 17 and up.   Groups up to 25 persons.
Days & Hours: By appointment.
Admission: Free.
Guided Tour: Lasts 2–5 hours depending on interest of group.
                  Write one month in advance. A list of names of
                  visitors must be submitted ahead of time.

MILK

Everyone knows that the cow is our real milk manufacturer, but did you know that she weighs about 1,200 pounds or that she drinks from 10 to 20 gallons of water a day?

A cow eats 21,000 pounds of feed a year in addition to two or more acres of pasture. In return she gives 3,500 quarts of milk annually. And did you know that she has four stomachs and that "cuds" are egg-size balls that she chews and chews?

This and other information is offered on a tour of any number of dairies in nearby Maryland or Virginia.

Maryland & Virginia Milk Producers Association
      (25–35 miles from D.C.)
P.O. Box 9154
Rosslyn Station
Arlington, Va. 22209. Tel. (703) 524-2300

Ages 6–12.   Groups only.

Days & Hours: By appointment.
Admission: Free.
Guided Tour: The above association does not give tours, but
                 will arrange a visit to a Maryland or Virginia milk
                 farm.

NEWSPAPERS

A visit to a newspaper is great fun for children, and is educational besides. Usually a tour covers the news department, business office, press and composing room, and mailing and circulation departments.

We have listed four newspapers: three dailies and a weekly.

1. The *Alexandria Gazette* was founded in 1784, making it the oldest daily newspaper published in the United States.

   Alexandria Gazette (5 miles from D.C.)
   717 N. St. Asaph Street
   Alexandria, Va. 22313. Tel. (703) 749-0004

   All ages.   Groups of 15–20 are preferred. Individuals may join
               scheduled tours.
   Days & Hours: By appointment.
   Admission: Free.
   Guided Tour: Write or telephone Jane Howard, Tour Informa-
                   tion. Visit lasts 45 minutes or longer.

2. *Washington Post*
   1150 15th Street, N.W.

Washington, D.C. 20005. Tel. 223-7737

Ages 12 and up.   Individuals & groups up to 30 persons.
Days & Hours: *By appointment.*
Admission: *Free.*
Guided Tour: *Lasts about one hour. Write or telephone in advance.*

3. *Washington Star*
225 Virginia Avenue, S.W.
Washington, D.C. 20003. Tel. 484-4132

Ages 12 and up.   Groups up to 30 persons. Individuals may join scheduled tour.
Days & Hours: *By appointment.*
Admission: *Free.*
Guided Tour: *Lasts one hour and includes a visit to the newsphoto lab. Telephone one week in advance.*

4. *The Sentinel* (30 miles from D.C.)
301 Comprint Lane
Gaithersburg, Md. 20860. Tel. (301) 948-1500, Ext. 68

Ages 8 and up.   Groups up to 30 persons. One adult to 10 children.
Days & Hours: *Thursday and Friday, by appointment.*
Admission: *Free.*
Guided Tour: *Lasts about one hour. The visit also focuses on career opportunities, such as journalism, art layout, etc. Write or telephone one week in advance.*

PHOTOGRAPHY

Everyone will learn something about photography on a group tour of the U.S. Naval Photographic Center.

This department is divided into three major sections: motion pictures, still photography, and research and development. The motion picture division is the largest, and makes documentaries for the Navy and other government agencies, including the White House.

Visitors tour the facilities and watch students and professional photographers at work.

U.S. Naval Photographic Center
Naval District Washington
Washington, D.C. 20374. Tel. 433-2159

Ages 13 and up.   Groups of 10 to 20 persons.
Days & Hours: *By appointment.*
Admission: *Free.*
Guided Tour: *Lasts 2–3 hours. Write or telephone ten days in advance.*

PIANOS

Did you ever see the "guts" of a piano? You may at Schaeffer's if you come there when a piano is being taken apart or put together or when new legs are being attached to an old body.

Visitors of all ages find a trip here fascinating. Come, browse, watch, ask questions.

Schaeffer's Piano Company
710 Sligo Avenue
Silver Spring, Md. 20910. Tel. (301) 589-3039

All ages.   Individuals & groups up to 10 persons.
Days & Hours: Monday–Friday 9:00–9:00. Saturday 9:00–6:00.
Guided Tour: By appointment.

POLICE DEPARTMENT

The tour begins in the communications department where incoming calls from trouble-shooting dispatchers first arrive and move to the Fire Arms Identification Section and the Line-Up Room.

Visitors are welcome to see the Police Department's Harbor Patrol Section if they can provide their own transportation. Five-year-olds and below will not be turned away, but the Police Department discourages this age level from taking the tour.

Metropolitan Police Department
Community Relations Division, Room 4121
300 Indiana Avenue, N.W.
Washington, D.C. 20001. Tel. 626-2600

All ages.   Individuals & groups.
Days & Hours: By appointment.
Admission: Free.
Guided Tour: Lasts about 1½ hours. Write or telephone in advance.

PRINTING

Take a fascinating, behind-the-scenes tour of these printing plants and see how type is set, the plates are made, and books and magazines are printed and bound.

1. Colortone Press also produces calendars, catalogues, and posters.

Colortone Press
2400 17th Street, N.W.
Washington, D.C. 20009. Tel. 387-6800, Ext. 53

Ages 12 and up.   Groups of 5–10 persons.
Days & Hours: By appointment.
Admission: Free.
Guided Tour: Write or telephone in advance.

2. Merkle Press specializes in the printing of magazines, including *Time, Sports Illustrated,* the *New Republic,* and others.

Merkle Press
810 Rhode Island Avenue, N.W.
Washington, D.C. 20018. Tel. 832-6420

Ages 10 and up. Groups only, but individuals may join a
                 scheduled tour.
Days & Hours: By appointment.
Admission: Free.
*Guided Tour: Lasts about 1½ hours. Write or telephone one
                 week in advance.*

SCHOOL FOR PAGES

It could only happen in Washington!

Plan a visit to the School for Pages, located in the Library of Congress. The school consists of 81 students who are Congressional pages and who attend classes equivalent to the 11th and 12th grades, or the last two years of high school. Classes start at 6:10 in the morning, and at 9:45 the students report for their jobs as pages.

Fifty-one of the pages work in the House of Representatives, twenty-six are assigned to Senators, and four work in the Supreme Court.

The rule that a Supreme Court page must not be taller than the high-backed chairs of the Justices or that girls are not eligible for these jobs is now outdated.

The students, twelve years of age and older, who are interested in becoming Congressional pages will find this visit especially exciting.

Capitol Page School
10 First Street, S.E.
Washington, D.C. 20540. Tel. 225-2021/2

Ages 12 and up.   Individuals or small groups.
Days & Hours: *By appointment. School is not in session during July and August, but facilities are open.*
Admission: *Free.*
Guided Tour: *Can be arranged by telephoning the principal's office.*

SCULPTURE IN GLASS

Herman Perlman is a genius in glass.

His subjects range from ballet dancers to studies of notables . . . including Pope John XXIII, Winston Churchill, Albert Einstein, Eleanor Roosevelt, and Martin Luther King, Jr. A life-size sculpture in glass of our 16th President stands in the Lincoln Birthplace Memorial at Hodgenville, Kentucky.

The artist's favorite themes are characters from the Bible and Jewish life, and he has immortalized in glass Moses on Mt. Sinai, Noah's Ark, a rejoicing Hassid, and others.

No tours are available and large groups cannot be accommodated, but individuals or small groups may come at the convenience of the artist.

Herman Perlman
950 Barry Place, N.W.
Washington, D.C. 20001. Tel. 265-9341

Ages 10 and up.   Individuals or small groups.
Days & Hours: By appointment.
Admission: Free.
Guided Tour: The artist will explain his work.

SKIN DIVING SCHOOL

Children of all ages are fascinated by this skin diving school where they can watch students take lessons and see the equipment that underwater enthusiasts use.

School manager Stuart Stinchfield teaches skin diving, goes "salvaging," has a font of knowledge on the "underwater world," and loves to talk about his findings. He'll be glad to answer questions when he's available.

Divers World Skin Diving School (½ mile from D.C.)
923 Gist Avenue
Silver Spring, Md. 20910. Tel. (301) 589-7564

Ages 12 and up.   Individuals & groups.
Days & Hours: Monday–Saturday 10:00–6:00.
Admission: Free.
Guided Tour: Not available.

TELEPHONE COMPANY

Even youngsters who are not scientifically-minded enjoy a visit to the Chesapeake & Potomac Telephone Company. Guides explain how the telephone works and how electronic equipment in central offices around the country makes it possible to dial one of more than 100 million telephones in the United States.

Visitors are shown the electronic switchboard, the long distance and assistance operators' offices, and the work centers.

Chesapeake & Potomac Telephone Co.
930 H Street, N.W.
Washington, D.C. 20001. Tel. 637-9900

Ages 8 and up.   Groups only.
Days & Hours: By appointment.

Admission:　　Free.
Guided Tour:　Write or telephone Ms. Anna Marie Lewis, public relations, two weeks in advance.

TELEVISION STUDIO TOURS

1. A guided tour of Station WTTG-TV shows how television images are produced and transmitted. Visitors can see a TV studio, the engineering control room, and possibly the taping of a show. Tours are geared to the age and interest levels of the group.

WTTG-TV Metromedia Television
5151 Wisconsin Avenue, N.W.
Washington, D.C. 20016. Tel. 244-5151, Ext. 366

Ages 7 and up.　Groups up to 20.
Days & Hours: By appointment.
Admission:　　Free.
Guided Tour:　Write or telephone one month in advance.

2. A tour to WMAL-TV includes a visit to two studios, the graphics department, and the news, wire service, and film editing rooms, with an explanation on how a film is produced.

WMAL-TV
4461 Connecticut Avenue, N.W.
Washington, D.C. 20008. Tel. 686-3000

All ages.　Groups only, but individuals may join scheduled tour.
Days & Hours: Monday–Friday. By appointment.
Admission:　　Free.

Guided Tour: *Telephone Public Service Dept. Ext. 3159 one week in advance.*

TOBACCO PLANTATION

The topic for visitors to the University of Maryland's Tobacco Experimental Farm is tobacco.

An expert explains how the leaf is grown, picked, and cured. The tour also includes a visit to the stripping room and a look at the leaves being made ready for market.

Plan to combine your trip with a visit to the tobacco auction warehouses in the immediate vicinity. The best months are usually April and May. For information write to the Farmers Tobacco Auction, Upper Marlboro, Maryland, 20870. Telephone: (301) 274-3124 or 3101.

Tobacco Experimental Farm (12 miles from D.C.)
2005 Fargo Road
Upper Marlboro, Md. 20870. Tel. (301) 627-3273

Ages 9 and up.   Groups only.
Days & Hours: By appointment.
Admission: Free.
Guided Tour: *Write or telephone one month in advance.*

WASHINGTON CITY POST OFFICE

A guided tour through the capital's main Post Office tells the story of the journey of a letter from the moment it is put in the mailbox until it reaches its destination. It shows how letters are culled, canceled, sorted, "trayed," packed, and sent off to the addressee. (Arrangements for similar tours can also be made with the neighborhood post offices.)

Washington City Post Office
North Capitol Street & Mass. Avenue, N.W.
Washington, D.C. 20013. Tel. 523-2031

Ages 8 and up.   Groups of 15–20 preferred. Individuals may join
                 scheduled tour.
Days & Hours: *Never closed except Christmas Day.*
Admission: *Free.*
Guided Tour: *By appointment. Telephone 523-2029 one to two*
                weeks in advance.

6 Technology and Modern Life

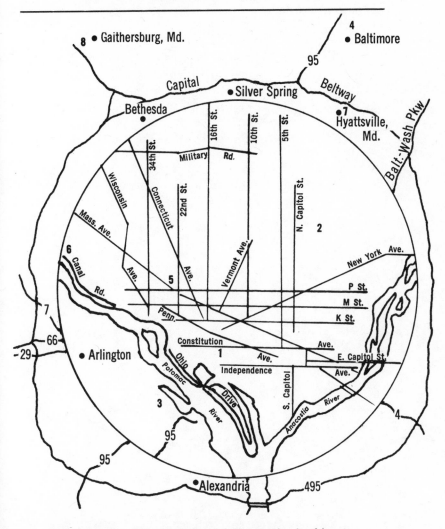

8 • Gaithersburg, Md.

4 • Baltimore

95

Capital

• Silver Spring

Beltway

Bethesda

16th St.

10th St.

5th St.

• 7 Hyattsville, Md.

Balt.-Wash Pkw

34th St.

Military Rd.

Wisconsin

Connecticut

22nd St.

N. Capitol St.

2

Mass. Ave.

Vermont Ave.

New York Ave.

6 Canal

Ave.

Ave.

5

P St.

Rd.

M St.

7

Penn.

K St.

66

Constitution

Ave.

– 29

• Arlington

1

Ave.

E. Capitol St.

Ohio

Independence

Ave.

Potomac

Drive

S. Capitol

3

River

Anacostia

River

4

95

95

• Alexandria

495

Note: Unless otherwise indicated, the entries in this section are at the Smithsonian Museum of History and Technology.

MAP LEGEND

1. Smithsonian Museum of History and Technology
2. Catholic University
3. U.S. Patent Office
4. Baltimore & Ohio Museum
5. The Textile Museum
6. Dalecarlia Water Treatment Plant
7. Washington Suburban Sanitary Commission
8. National Bureau of Standards

BRIDGES AND TUNNELS

1. An exhibit of bridge and tunnel construction, from ancient times to the present. Models illustrate the development of various types of bridges, including the famous Brooklyn Bridge.

2. One of the finest collections of model bridges in the country can be found in the Baltimore and Ohio Transportation Museum. See *Railroads* (page 121).

CHEMISTRY LABORATORIES

At the Museum of History and Technology, two chemistry laboratories of the past illustrate the progress of science.

The first is the 18th-century workshop of Joseph Priestley, the British theologian and scientist who discovered oxygen but failed to grasp its significance. The second is a more modern laboratory, dating back to the late 19th century.

CLOCKS AND CHRONOMETERS

Clock lovers of all ages will enjoy the fascinating display at the Smithsonian. The story of measuring time and of the instruments used is traced from sundials and water-clocks to mechanical timepieces.

Visitors will see astronomical time-measuring equipment, atomic clocks, and the re-created workshop of William Cranch Bond, the 19th-century Boston astronomer who was famous for designing ship chronometers.

COMPUTERS AND DATA PROCESSING DEVICES

Future computer scientists will be interested in the adding and calculating machines and the various data processing devices in the Physical Sciences and Mathematics Section.

ELECTRICITY

Working demonstration-models of laser and maser beams are among the displays illustrating the development and application of theories of electricity.

Here is where the scientists of tomorrow can observe and study the contributions to science made by Benjamin Franklin, Michael Faraday, and others.

ELECTRONIC COMMUNICATIONS

The radio, the telephone, the telegraph, and other marvels of electronic communication are exhibited at the Museum of History and Technology. Recent developments in radar and radio astronomy are explained, and a small, up-to-date library on the subject is open to the public.

FARM MACHINERY

City-bred youngsters in particular are fascinated by the extensive scale models and farming implements describing agriculture through the centuries. Exhibits show tools and equipment ranging from the wooden plow to the modern power machinery farmers use today.

GLASS FOR SAFETY

Science-oriented students 12 years of age and above will be thrilled to visit Catholic University's Vitreous State Laboratory. Here physicists are trying to make glass safer as well as to find new uses for it in our everyday life.

One of their latest discoveries is glass for windowshields that will turn into a powdered substance on impact.

The Catholic University of America
620 Michigan Avenue, N.E.
Washington, D.C. 20017. Tel. 635-5600

Ages 12 and up.   Groups only.
Days & Hours: By appointment.
Admission: Free.

Guided Tour: *Can be arranged. Telephone two to three weeks in advance.*

INSTRUMENTS OF SCIENCE AND TECHNOLOGY

If you are interested in learning the origin of things, you will find it fascinating to see instruments from the primitive Persian sextant and the early abacus calculator right up to the latest electronic computers.

Exhibits also show meteorological and seismological apparatus, and highlight the use of instruments in explorations.

INSTRUMENTS OF SOUND

Young visitors are fascinated by the Smithsonian's assemblage of sound instruments which include Edison's 1877 phonograph, Berliner's gramophone of 1888, and the Victor Talking Machine.

IRON AND STEEL

This Smithsonian exhibit explains how iron has been smelted in colonial days on an open hearth to the present, when the operation takes place in a modern, complex steel mill.

NUCLEAR ENERGY

Even if you don't know the difference between uranium and Uranus, the science-fictionish equipment here is exciting.

On display is the Dunning cyclotron that first split the atom in the United States and the Figure-8 stellarator used by astrophysicist Lyman Spitzer in his controlled nuclear fusion work at Princeton in 1951.

It all looks puzzling to the old folks, but space-minded youngsters have a field day.

PATENTS

1. Most of the original patent models have been transferred from the Patent Office to the Museum of History and Technology. However, a limited number of the early models are on view at this office—along with files of more than 3.7 million patents.

The tour includes a visit to the Public Search Room and a talk by a staff member, followed by a question-and-answer period.

United States Patent Office (3 miles from D.C.)
2021 Jefferson Davis Highway
Arlington, Va. 20231. Tel. (703) 557-3428

Ages 12 and up.   Individuals & groups.
Days & Hours: Monday–Friday 8:30–5:00.
Admission: Free.
Guided Tour: *By appointment only. Telephone two to three weeks in advance.*

2. The collection of patents transferred from the Patent Office to the Museum of History and Technology includes models of Elias Howe's sewing machine and Edison's phonograph.

PETROLEUM

The story of petroleum and the importance of the petrochemical industry in modern society is presented in the Museum of History and Technology. The exhibit explains the methods and equipment used to discover, drill, recover, refine, and transport petroleum.

POWER MACHINERY

This Smithsonian exhibit traces man's attempts and final success in harnessing power and developing tools for greater speed and efficiency.

It shows the use of the early waterwheel and the developments leading to the present hydroelectric turbines.

Many models are in working condition, and will operate at the push of a button.

PRINTING

The miracle of printing is shown here, from early hand presses to the most modern machinery.

Visitors can see Benjamin Franklin's printing press, an early type foundry, a full-scale Japanese woodcutting shop, and a variety of materials used in drawing, printing, and writing, along with demonstrations of the printing process.

RAILROADS

1. The railroad display, with its chugs, hoots, whistles, and thundering engines, is one of the most popular in the Smithsonian.

Young boys love the Southern Railway's Pacific-type passenger engine. Here is the cable car of 1888 from Seattle; the 1836, 8-wheel passenger car, the oldest in existence; a diorama of New York's Third Avenue "El" as it looked in 1880; and Moses Farmer's 1847 electric locomotive.

The museum also has a fascinating collection of scale models showing the development of rail transportation.

2. The history of railroads and other means of travel comes alive in the Baltimore and Ohio Transportation Museum.

It's the largest institution of railroad equipment in America, and among its treasured exhibits is a replica of the famous Tom Thumb steam-powered vehicle built by Peter Cooper in 1829. Visitors may also see an ancient fire engine, model railroads, and the railroad tools used to lay the groundwork for a modern nation.

A popular display is the collection of freight cars, cabooses, locomotives, primitive cars, Conestoga wagons, and other vehicles on wheels.

Baltimore & Ohio Museum (40 miles from D.C.)
900 W. Pratt Street
Baltimore, Md. 21223. Tel. (301) 237-2381

All ages.   Individuals & groups.
Days & Hours: Wednesday–Sunday 10:00–4:00. Closed holidays.
Admission: Children: $.50.   Adults: $1.00.
Guided Tour: Groups should write or telephone one week in advance.

ROTATION OF THE EARTH

The large hanging Foucault Pendulum in the Museum of History and Technology demonstrates the rotation of the earth. Suspended 71½ feet from the museum's fourth floor ceiling to the first floor, it swings back and forth knocking down red markers arranged in a circle.

This remarkable pendulum was designed by the famed 19th-century French physicist Léon Foucault, known for his research in astronomy and the speed of light. Foucault's Pendulum is the first credible method demonstrating the principle of the rotation of the earth.

TELESCOPE MAKER

Especially interesting to telescope-minded young people is a visit to the fascinating shop of Henry Fitz, an

18th-century telescope maker. View the observatory where a lifelike Mr. Fitz sits at his worktable, surrounded by the actual shelves and tools he used.

TEXTILES—MACHINERY AND MUSEUM

1. Machines that changed textile-making from a family operation to a major world industry are on display here. They include Samuel Slater's 1790 carding machine; the Jacquard loom, the first machine to weave in patterns; and the patent models for the Bigelow carpet loom.

Embroidery and needlework are featured, and experts demonstrate the techniques of hand-spinning and weaving.

Inquire about demonstration schedules.

2. Over 9,000 varieties of woven fabrics and rugs are shown in the Textile Museum. The only museum of its kind in this country, it contains ancient fabrics from faraway lands.

There are floor coverings from the Near East; fabrics from Spain and Portugal and their former African colonies; and fine examples of hand-weaving from Asia, Africa, and the Americas.

The Museum has gallery talks, lectures, and occasional demonstrations by craftsmen.

The Textile Museum
2320 S Street, N.W.

Washington, D.C. 20008. Tel. 667-0442

All ages.   Individuals & groups.
Days & Hours: *Tuesday–Saturday 10:00–5:00, Sunday 1:00–5:00.*
                Closed Christmas and New Year's.
Admission: *Children: Free. Adults: Voluntary contribution*
                optional.
Guided Tour: *For groups. Write or telephone two weeks in*
                advance. Individuals may join scheduled tour.

TOOLS

The history of tools, from ancient times to the present, is documented in an exhibit at the Museum of History and Technology. Major attractions are a typical machine shop of the mid-19th century and an exhibit of machinery from the early 1900s to the present.

Demonstrations show tools at work.

WATER PURIFICATION

1. How can the polluted Potomac River water be made fit to drink?

A visit to the Dalecarlia Water Treatment Plant will reveal the process. This modern plant filtrates, purifies, and chemically controls the water in the District of Columbia and suburban Washington.

School tours are available for 7th graders and above with occasional "open house" sessions for families.

Filmstrips explain the story of water.

Dalecarlia Water Treatment Plant
5900 MacArthur Blvd., N.W.
Washington, D.C. 20315. Tel. 282-2753

Ages 12 and up.   Groups only.
Days & Hours: *By appointment only.*
Admission: *Free.*
Guided Tour: *Lasts one hour. Write or telephone 282-2701 in*
                 advance.

2. Fifth graders and above can learn about current water supply and waste disposal problems during a visit to the Washington Suburban Sanitary Commission's regional water filtration plants.

The Commission will reimburse the Board of Education for transportation costs incurred by local classes visiting the plant during the school year.

Visits include a conducted tour of the area, a slide show, a lecture, and a question-and-answer period.

Washington Suburban Sanitary Commission
4017 Hamilton Street
Hyattsville, Md. 20781. Tel. (301) 277-7700, Ext. 489 or
    224

Ages 12 and up.   Groups up to 40 persons.
Days & Hours: *By appointment.*
Admission: *Free.*
Guided Tour: *Write at least three weeks in advance and give*
                 alternate dates.

WEIGHTS AND MEASUREMENTS

The world's largest measurement laboratory is housed in a 21-building complex on 570 acres of land.

The National Bureau of Standards provides basic standards for measuring length, time, mass, temperature, etc.

A staff of scientists is engaged in research and development in chemistry, engineering, and physics, and assists in solving technological problems. For example, the National Bureau of Standards will play a major role in America's conversion to the metric system.

The Bureau's museum includes displays of scientific apparatus, important memorabilia, and historic documents concerning the science of measurement.

Junior high school students and older, with an interest in the physical sciences, would benefit most by visiting the Bureau's measurement and testing laboratories and museum.

National Bureau of Standards (20 miles from D.C.) Gaithersburg, Md. 20234. Tel. (301) 921-2721

Ages 12 and up.   Individuals & groups.
Days & Hours: *By appointment.*
Admission: *Free.*
Guided Tour: *Tuesday at 1:30 P.M. and Friday 9:30 A.M. Write or telephone one week in advance.*

7 Collections and Exhibits

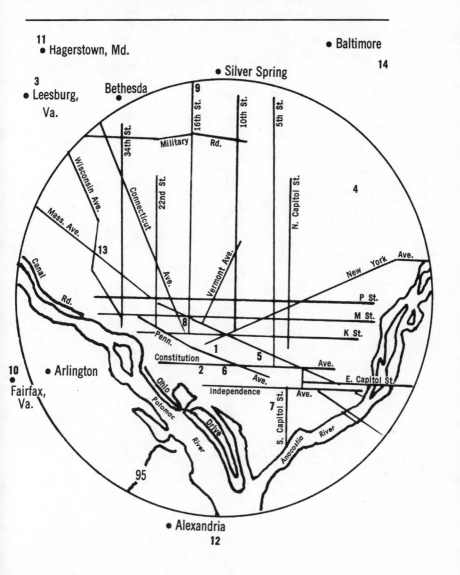

MAP LEGEND

1. Old Antique House
2. Smithsonian Museum of History and Technology
3. Carriage Museum
4. Franciscan Monastery
5. National Collection of Fine Arts
6. Smithsonian Museum of Natural History
7. National Historical Wax Museum and Dolphinarium
8. B'nai B'rith Exhibit Hall
9. Armed Forces Medical Museum
10. Fairhill Farm Antiques
11. M. P. Möller Organ Co.
12. George Washington Masonic Memorial
13. Washington Cathedral
14. U.S. Army Ordnance Museum

ANTIQUE HOUSE

The largest and oldest antique shop in the Washington area is a five-story building filled with valuable pieces of furniture and accessories going back to the days of Charles II of England.

Old Antique House
817 Pennsylvania Avenue, N.W.
Washington, D.C. 20004. Tel. 628-5640

All ages.   Individuals & groups.
Days & Hours: Monday–Friday 9:00–5:00, Saturday 9:30–4:00. *Closed Thanksgiving, Christmas, and New Year's.*
Admission: Free.
Guided Tour: Not available. Large groups should call in advance.

CAROUSEL

It is hard to tear children away from this Smithsonian exhibit. The little ones are hypnotized by the round-and-round motion of the revolving ring of wooden animals. Some children have eyes only for the colorful goat, others follow the rotating elephant, and the very young are smitten by the spangle-glittered horse.
• At the Smithsonian Museum of History and Technology.

CARRIAGE MUSEUM

Visitors to the famous Morven Estate carriage house, turned into a museum in 1969, may hitch a horse to a carriage and take an exciting ride around the expansive estate.

More than 75 horse-drawn vehicles, restored to excellent condition, are on exhibit. Included are buggies, sulkies, sleighs, phaetons, a landau, an opera, a red-and-brass fire engine pumper, and a display of miniature models.

The colorful sport of "coaching," or driving horse-drawn vehicles, is becoming a popular pastime, and may be observed here during the annual fall "coaching-day" event.

Also see School for Riders, Chapter 4 (page 79).

Carriage Museum at Morven Park (35 miles from D.C.)
Route #2, Box 50
Leesburg, Va. 22075. Tel. (703) 777-2414

Ages 6 and up.   Individuals & groups.
Days & Hours: Tuesday–Saturday 10:00–5:00; Sunday 1:00–5:00. Closed Mondays, holidays, and November through March.
Admission: Children: $.75. Adults: $1.75.
Guided Tour: Through the mansion. Large groups should write or telephone in advance.

CATACOMBS

The Franciscan Monastery has a reproduction of the catacombs in Rome where Christians hid and worshipped in secret during the age of persecution.

There is also a reproduction of the Grotto of Bethlehem, the Altar of Calvary, and the Grotto of Lourdes.

Franciscan Monastery
1400 Quincy Street, N.E.
Washington, D.C. 20017. Tel. 526-6800

All ages. Individuals & groups.
Days & Hours: Open daily 8:00–5:00.
Admission: Voluntary contribution.
Guided Tour: Every 45 minutes, beginning 8:30 A.M.

CHILDREN'S GALLERY

The National Collection of Fine Arts in the historic Patent Office Building is one of Washington's top attractions.

Its Children's Gallery, a great favorite with the young set, has a miniature door leading the way to fascinating exhibits hung at children's eye-level.

A program particularly geared to elementary school children from kindergarten through sixth grade is the "Improvisational Tours." These presentations provide an opportunity for children to "act out" verbally and bodily what they see in a canvas or in a piece of sculpture. Another special feature is the annual "Children's Day" which takes place in mid-May each year.

National Collection of Fine Arts
9th & G Streets, N.W.
Washington, D.C. 20560. Tel. 381-6541/2

All ages.   Individuals & groups.
Days & Hours: Daily 10:00–5:30. Closed Christmas.
Admission: Free.
*Guided Tour: For "Improvisational Tours" telephone or write
                at least ten days in advance. Groups of less than
                30 preferred.*

DOLL'S HOUSE

Children of all ages are attracted to this exhibit, as are many adults. This large doll's house with more than twenty rooms filled with all sorts of grown-up furnishings in miniature size includes parlors, bedrooms, guest rooms, a fish tank for the living room, and a typewriter in the study.

• At the Smithsonian Museum of History and Technology.

GEMS AND MINERALS

The Halls of Mineral Sciences at the Museum of Natural History house one of the finest collections of gems and minerals in the world. It includes the 330-carat sapphire known as the Star of India and the famous Hope Diamond, the largest blue diamond in the world.

Legend has it that the fabulous Hope Diamond, brought from India to France in 1668, weighed 68 carats and became part of the crown jewels of Louis XIV. It was stolen during the French Revolution, and in 1830 a 44-carat blue diamond appeared that was presumed to have been cut from the missing gem in King Louis' collection.

The stone was purchased by an Englishman named Henry Thomas Hope, and after many adventures it was purchased by the prominent New York jeweler Harry Winston who presented the mystery-laden diamond to the Smithsonian.

• At the Smithsonian Museum of Natural History.

GLASS MAKING

The story of glass and how it is made, from earliest time to the present, is highlighted in an exhibit at the Smithsonian. The collection includes Egyptian and Roman glass, cut crystal from England, 18th-century American Stiegel and Amelung, 19th-century Tiffany, and exquisite 20th-century Steuben and Swedish glass.

• At the Smithsonian Museum of History and Technology.

HISTORY IN WAX

At this museum, lifelike figures and scenes in wax re-create history and portray patriots, scientists, and space-age heroes.

Christopher Columbus is here, along with young John Kennedy and his sister Caroline, and Neil Armstrong standing on the moon.

Press a button and hear historic words or see Moses on Mount Sinai holding the Ten Commandments. And there is a Dolphinarium with scheduled performances by trained dolphins.

National Historical Wax Museum & Dolphinarium
333 E Street, S.W.
Washington, D.C. 20024. Tel. 554-2600

All ages.   Individuals & groups.
Days & Hours: March–Labor Day 9:00–10:00. Other times 9:00–
8:00. Closed Christmas.
Admission: *Children: $1.25. Adults: $2.00. Special group*
rates. Additional entrance fee to the Dolphin-
arium.

JEWISH ART AND HISTORY

The B'nai B'rith Exhibit Hall houses ancient and modern Jewish ceremonial art objects and the historic letter George Washington wrote to the Newport, Rhode Island, Hebrew Congregation.

There are also changing exhibits of contemporary painting and sculpture on Jewish themes and an extensive library of Jewish Americana.

B'nai B'rith Exhibit Hall
1640 Rhode Island Avenue, N.W.
Washington, D.C. 20036. Tel. 393-5284, Ext. 203

All ages.   Individuals & groups.
Days & Hours: Monday–Friday 9:00–5:00, Sunday 10:00–5:00.
                     Closed Jewish and national holidays.
Admission: *Free.*
Guided Tour: *By appointment. Write or telephone in advance.*

MEDICINE

1. The art of healing is traced from its earliest beginnings in magic to modern open-heart surgery. Displays feature anaesthetic and biological laboratories of the middle 19th century, one of the first iron lungs, and other life-saving devices.
• At the Smithsonian Museum of History and Technology.

2. This medical museum is devoted to the study of human and animal diseases, war-related injuries, and current social and medical problems, such as drug abuse, smoking, etc.
Its collection of microscopes is the most comprehensive in the world.

Armed Forces
Institute of Pathology Medical Museum
6825 16th Street, N.W.
Washington, D.C. 20306. Tel. (301) 576-3232

All ages.   Individuals & groups.
Days & Hours: Daily except Christmas 9:00–5:00.

Admission: Free.
Guided Tour: By appointment. Write or telephone two weeks in advance.

(Temporarily housing the University of Health Sciences, the Museum is closed until November 1, 1976.)

MONEY AND MEDALS

1. Everyone is fascinated by money; everyone loves it. And here is a chance to find out where it started, how it evolved from the primitive bartering with beads, seashells, and furs to our present complex monetary system.

In the section History of Money, the Smithsonian has displays ranging from the lumpy-looking Lydian coin of 65 B.C. to the $100,000 bill bearing the image of President Wilson. On exhibit are English groats, Bohemian ducats, and the original foot-high artist's model for the Kennedy half-dollar.

Always popular is the special children's corner and the Gold Room housing the Josiah K. Lilly Collection of gold medals.

• At the Smithsonian Museum of History and Technology.

2. Money comes in many shapes, and the Smithsonian's Museum of Natural History has a unique and mysterious large circular stone with a hole in the center from Yap, in the Caroline Islands, east of the Philippines—once used as money.

• At the Smithsonian Museum of Natural History.

NOSTALGIA

A fascinating collection of "nostalgia" can be viewed at Fairhill Farm Antiques. Barns are filled with horsedrawn carriages and old automobiles, including the First Model A. There is also the original RCA Victor Dog, a collection of barbershop poles, and more than 200 musical instruments of various types.

Favorites among the young are antique jukeboxes, hand and pump organs, mechanically-played banjos, harps, violins, pianos, and amusement park equipment. Why, there are even early popcorn machines.

Fairhill Farm Antiques (9 miles from D.C.)
8731 Lee Highway
Fairfax, Va. 22030. Tel. (703) 560-2846

All ages.   Groups of 3–40.
Days & Hours: *By appointment.*
Admission: *Free.*
Guided Tour: *Lasts about one hour. Write or telephone three weeks in advance.*

PHOTOGRAPHY

At the Smithsonian, camera fans have a unique opportunity to view the world's greatest variety of photographic equipment, from the early still cameras and motion picture units to today's motorized equipment.

Catch glimpses of an early photographic studio, a very

primitive darkroom, and a gallery with changing photographic exhibits. The story of photography's role in modern times is vividly explained. A must for photo buffs of all ages.

• At the Smithsonian Museum of History and Technology.

PIPE ORGANS

The organ is a musical instrument equipped with a keyboard in which air is forced across reeds (reed organ) or through graduated pipes (pipe organ).

A visit to the M. P. Möller Pipe Organ Company, the largest manufacturer of pipe organs in the world, is an awe-inspiring experience. A tour shows visitors the many steps that go into the making of this often heard but little known instrument whose heritage goes back to the second century B.C.

Visits are limited to music-interested high school seniors, college students, and professional musicians. A short talk on the pipe organ may be requested in advance.

M. P. Möller Organ Company (70 miles from D.C.)
403 N. Prospect Street
Hagerstown, Md. 21740. Tel. (301) 733-9000

Ages: See above.   Groups only.
Days & Hours: By appointment.
Admission: Free.
Guided Tour: Write or telephone in advance.

POTTERS AND CERAMISTS

Striking examples of pottery and ceramics from earliest times to the present are displayed in a series of galleries at the Museum of History and Technology. The last gallery features creations of contemporary American artists-craftsmen, and an absorbing and informative documentary film shows ceramists and potters at work.

• At the Smithsonian Museum of History and Technology.

SHRINERS ON PARADE

The George Washington Masonic National Memorial, where our first President served as the Master of the Lodge, is a treasure trove for Washington buffs.

On display is the small trowel that Washington used to lay the cornerstone of the Capitol in 1793, his family Bible, and his famous bedroom clock, reputed to have stopped at 10:20 P.M. on December 14, 1799, the moment of his death.

The eighth floor chapel has a collection of knights in armor, banners, swords, and pikes that fascinates children.

The Observatory floor gives a panoramic view of Washington, and the special exhibit that delights all viewers, but especially children, is the collection of mechanical toy Shriners in colorful uniforms who march in formation with musical accompaniment at the press of a button.

George Washington Masonic National Memorial
        (8 miles from D.C.)
King Street & Callaway Drive
Alexandria, Va. 22301. Tel. (703) 683-2007

All ages.   Individuals & groups.
Days & Hours: Every day 9:00–5:00. Closed Thanksgiving, Christmas, New Year's.
Admission: Free.
Guided Tour: 9:15–4:15. Tour lasts one hour. For large groups write or telephone Marvin Fowler, Executive Secretary.

SKULLS AND SKELETONS

If you like bones you'll adore the Museum of Natural History's collection of skeletons of most of the creatures in the world, including many you have probably never even heard of.

Skeletons of birds, reptiles, fishes, and bone structures of man and beast are displayed. Illuminating exhibits illustrate the relationships and differences between man and beast.

• At the Smithsonian Museum of Natural History.

STAINED GLASS

Washington Cathedral's stained glass windows are masterpieces of color and design. The glass comes from England, France, Germany, and the United States.

Stop at the Children's Chapel, where everything is designed in miniature, including the stained glass windows illustrating familiar Bible stories.

A display and explanation of how stained glass is made can be found in the Cathedral's gift shop.

Washington Cathedral
Massachusetts & Wisconsin Avenues, N.W.
Washington, D.C. 20016. Tel. 966-3500, Ext. 249

All ages.   Individuals & groups.
Days & Hours: Every day 9:00–5:00.
Admission: Voluntary contribution.
Guided Tour: Throughout the day. Only groups need write or telephone for reservations, preferably one month in advance.

STAMPS AND THE MAILS

The history of the mail service is outlined here, from the early Sumerian clay tablets of 2500 B.C., which were carried by the king's messenger, to the rocket and missile mail of today.

In the National Postage Stamp Collection, stamp collectors will be delighted with the huge assortment of stamps from all parts of the world, housed in hundreds of glass-covered frames that slide out from the wall for viewing.

• At the Smithsonian Museum of History and Technology.

WEAPONS

1. The story of weapons from stone-age times to the present is told here. Extensive collections include such historic firearms as the original patent models of the Colt revolver, the Browning machine gun, and the Remington rifle.

Armored vehicles, missiles, and tanks are also displayed, with explanations given of their parts and usage.

• At the Smithsonian Museum of History and Technology.

2. The U.S. Army Ordnance Museum houses the world's most complete collection of American and foreign arms and ammunition. Rifles, mortars, artillery, armored vehicles, rockets, and missiles are exhibited here.

Established in 1919, the museum is a source to researchers and design engineers.

U.S. Army Ordnance Museum (60 miles from D.C.) Aberdeen Proving Grounds, Md. 21005. Tel. (301) 278-3602

Ages 8 and up.   Individuals & groups.
Days & Hours: Tuesday–Friday 12:00–5:00. Weekends 10:00–5:00.
Admission: *Free.*
Guided Tour: *By appointment. Telephone (301) 278-3581 or write: Information Officer, Office of the Secretary, USAO & C, two weeks in advance.*

8 Music, Sports, Theatricals

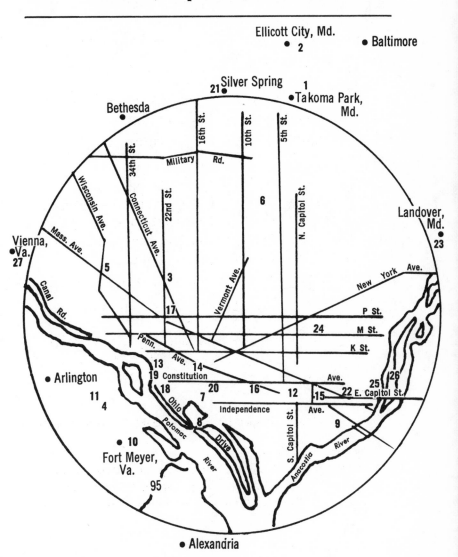

Ellicott City, Md.
• 2

• Baltimore

21• Silver Spring   1
• Takoma Park,
Md.

Bethesda •

16th St.

10th St.

5th St.

34th St.

Military   Rd.

Wisconsin Ave.

Connecticut Ave.

22nd St.

6

N. Capitol St.

Landover,
Md.
• 23

Mass. Ave.

Vienna,
• Va.
27

5

3

Vermont Ave.

New York   Ave.

Canal   Rd.

17

P St.

24   M St.

Penn.   Ave.

K St.

13   14

19   Constitution   Ave.

• Arlington   18   20   16   12   15

11   7   22 E. Capitol St.
4   25   26

Ohio   Independence   Ave.

8   9

Potomac   Drive

• 10   S. Capitol St.
Fort Meyer,
Va.   River   Anacostia   River

95

• Alexandria

MAP LEGEND

1. Kiddieland Park
2. Enchanted Forest
3. The National Ballet Company
4. Netherlands Carillon
5. Washington Cathedral
6. Washington Fencers Club
7. Washington Monument
8. Jefferson Memorial
9. Marine Barracks
10. Fort Meyer
11. Marine Corps War Memorial
12. The Capitol
13. American Film Institute
14. Corcoran Gallery
15. Library of Congress
16. National Gallery of Art
17. Phillips Collection
18. Lincoln Memorial
19. JFK Opera House
20. Smithsonian Museum of History and Technology
21. Dale Music Co.
22. Folger Shakespeare Library
23. Capital Centre
24. Washington Coliseum
25. National Guard Armory
26. RFK Memorial Stadium
27. Wolf Trap Farm Park

AMUSEMENT PARKS

Here are a few playgrounds and storybook places enjoyed by youngsters of all ages:

1. Kiddieland Park (½ mile from D.C.)
   6873 New Hampshire Avenue
   Takoma Park, Md. 20012. Tel. (301) 270-1434

   Ages 2–12. Individuals & groups.
   Days & Hours: Daily June–Labor Day and weekends during spring and fall.
   Admission: *Free. Rides are ten cents.*
   Guided Tour: Not available.

   Assorted amusement park rides are available.

2. Enchanted Forest (30 miles from D.C.)
   10040 Baltimore National Pike
   Ellicott City, Md. 21043. Tel. (301) 465-0707

   All ages. Individuals & groups.
   Days & Hours: Daily May 15–September 15 and weekends until end of October. 10:00–5:00.
   Admission: Children under 12: $.80.   Adults: $1.35.
   Guided Tour: Not available. Large groups should write or telephone two weeks in advance.

   Special features are: Safari ride, Cinderella Castle, Gingerbread House, etc.

BACKSTAGE AT THE BALLET

Going backstage to see a ballerina at arm's length adds to the thrill of the performance.

The National Ballet Company's productions are performed at the Opera House of the John F. Kennedy Center for the Performing Arts, and backstage visits may be arranged through the National Ballet Company office.

Performances of the "Nutcracker Ballet," however, take place each Christmas season at the Lisner Auditorium, and backstage visits may be arranged through the Lisner management (21 & H Streets, N.W., Tel. 676-6800).

Consult newspapers for performance schedules and ticket prices.

The National Ballet Company
2801 Connecticut Avenue, N.W.
Washington, D.C. 20008. Tel. 387-5544

All ages.   Individuals & small groups.
Days & Hours: Consult newspapers for ballet schedules.
Admission: With ticket to performance.
Guided Tour: Write or telephone two weeks in advance.

BELLS

The story of bells began most likely when early man first struck dishes or metal pots as a warning signal, for amusement or for distant communication.

Bells are perennially interesting, and the following are a few of the best known bells in the Washington area:

1. Given to America by the Dutch in gratitude for our help to them during World War II, the Netherlands

Carillon, with its 127-foot square tower containing 49 bells, stands as a symbol of friendship between the two countries.

The largest or "bourdon" bell weighs 12,654 pounds and measures over 6 feet in diameter. The smallest, 9 inches in diameter, weighs 37½ pounds.

The large bells represent the adults of the Netherlands; the small ones symbolize the country's youth.

Concerts by outstanding carillonneurs are presented on weekends and holidays.

Netherlands Carillon is located near the U.S. Marine Corps War Memorial and close to the Arlington National Cemetery. Concerts are held every Sunday at 3 P.M. and on February 22nd, May 5th, May 30th, July 4th, and November 11th.

2. The 301-foot belltower atop the Washington Cathedral has a 53-bell carillon weighing 60 tons. It also houses a ring of 10 bells, the only one of its kind in the world.

The carillon is played weekdays from 12:15 to 12:45, and the ring is played Sundays and holidays.

Visitors are not permitted to the top of the belltower.

Washington Cathedral
Massachusetts & Wisconsin Avenues, N.W.
Washington, D.C. 20016. Tel. 966-3500

BOOMERANGING

The history of the boomerang goes back to ancient Egypt and to other countries around the world where it was used in hunting and warfare. To this day it is closely identified with the natives of Australia.

It is also a sport of skill, and the secret is to throw the curved piece of wood so that it swerves in flight and returns to the exact spot where the thrower is standing.

Each year, in late spring, the Smithsonian holds an open tournament on the grounds of the Washington Monument. The contest is preceded by instructions in making and throwing the boomerang. The tournament is free, but there is a nominal fee for instructions. For further details communicate with:

Smithsonian Associates
Smithsonian Institution
Washington, D.C. 20560. Tel. 381-5157

Ages 9 and up.   Individuals & groups.

FENCING

Anyone interested in the art or practice of fencing can observe lessons for beginners or competitions between professionals at the Washington Fencers Club.

Visitors are welcome, but don't get too close to the action.

Washington Fencers Club
Petworth Methodist Church
New Hampshire Avenue & Upshur Street, N.W.
Washington, D.C. 20011. Tel. 783-2225

Ages 10 and up.   Individuals only.
Days & Hours: *Tuesdays and Thursdays 6:45–9:45 P.M. Closed*
national holidays.
Admission: *Free.*
Guided Tour: *Not available.*

JOUSTING

Jousting, a contest on horseback, is said to be the oldest horse-mounted sport in the world. Introduced in the United States in the early 17th century by Lord Baltimore, it became a favorite pastime of the early settlers, and is now Maryland's official state sport. In this fast-moving and colorful event, each rider wears a costume resembling the knights of old.

Maryland has many jousting contests during the year, and its National Jousting Tournaments Association together with the Washington National Capital Parks Service sponsors jousting contests on the grounds of the Washington Monument, usually during the month of October.

Check the newspapers or call the National Park Service (Tel. 426-6700) for scheduled tournaments.

Washington Monument Grounds
The Mall between 15th & 17th Streets, N.W.

KITE FLYING

Kite flying is a sport practiced in all parts of the world. In Washington the Smithsonian Associates, often in association with the National Capital Parks, presents the Annual Kite Carnival each mid-March or early April.

The contest attracts participants of all ages and from all walks of life who gather on the grounds of the Washington Monument to do their thing with kites.

For additional information call 381-5157.

MILITARY BANDS AND CEREMONIES

Military band music along with the bands' impressive drills and ceremonies are always great fun. Here are a few bands in the Washington area:

1. The Torchlight Tattoo is performed at the Jefferson Memorial by the Army Band on Wednesdays, from June through August at 8 P.M. Free.

2. Striking military ceremonies take place at the Marine Barracks at 8th and I Streets, S.E., on Friday from May through September. The ceremonies start evenings at 8:30 with a concert, and are followed by a drill at 9. Free, but advance seating reservations are a must.

3. Fort Meyer, in nearby Virginia, puts on parades on many Sunday afternoons at 4 P.M. Check beforehand by calling (on weekdays) 697-3366.

4. The Marine Corps War Memorial (the Iwo Jima Statue) is the scene of military ceremonies on Tuesday evenings at 7:30 P.M., from June through August.

5. The Army, Navy, Air Force, and Marine Corps bands give concerts on the East Front of the Capitol. Weekdays except Thursdays at 8 P.M. Spectators sit on the steps. June through August. Free.

MOVIES, OLD AND NEW

Exciting old movies, children's classics and many new films are shown at the 224-seat American Film Institute Theatre in the John F. Kennedy Center for the Performing Arts.

> American Film Institute Theatre
> 2700 F Street, N.W.
> Washington, D.C. 20566. Tel. 833-9300
>
> *Admission:*   *Children: $.50.   Adults: $.75.   Entrance fee subject to change.*

MUSIC

Washington offers musical enjoyment for every taste, with a large number of concerts free for the listening:

1. The National Symphony Orchestra of course ranks on

top, and besides its yearly subscription performances at the Kennedy Center, it offers a series of free concerts in the parks during the summer that are especially suitable for children.

Watch the newspapers for schedules or call the National Symphony Orchestra, Kennedy Center for the Performing Arts (Tel. 785-8100).

2. Corcoran Gallery, 17th Street at New York Avenue, N.W. (Tel. 638-3211). Chamber music concerts Sunday at 2:30 P.M. between October and May. Free.

3. Library of Congress, Independence Avenue at First Street, S.E. Offers a variety of concerts. Call (723-2211) for schedule and ticket information.

4. National Gallery of Art, Constitution Avenue at 6th Street, N.W. (Tel. 737-4215). The National Gallery Orchestra, chamber music groups, and other artists perform here on Sundays at 7:00 P.M. Mid-September through mid-June. Free.

5. Phillips Collection, 1600 21st Street, N.W. (Tel. 387-2151). Chamber music and song recitals, Sundays at 5:00 P.M. October through May. Free.

6. Watergate Concerts. The D.C. Recreation Symphony and military bands perform by the Potomac River near the Lincoln Memorial nightly from June through August at 8:30 P.M. Rent a canoe or rowboat and listen to a concert from the water. For more information call 629-7226.

7. Opera: Four productions are staged each year by the Opera Society of Washington. Performances are held at the JFK Opera House.

See "Bells" and "Military Bands," in this section.

MUSICAL INSTRUMENTS

1. Lovers of fine music will be enraptured by the Smithsonian collection of 18th- and 19th-century European instruments restored to excellent playing condition.
   Visitors can relax in a stereophonic chair, listen to music recorded on antique instruments, view a slide-and-sound documentary, and often hear performances in the chamber-music hall.
• At the Smithsonian Museum of History and Technology.

2. Visitors to the Dale Music Company can view a fine collection of antique and rare musical instruments. David Burchuk, musicologist and owner of the collection, will .explain and demonstrate the different instruments.

Dale Music Company, Inc. (5 miles from D.C.)
8240 Georgia Avenue
Silver Spring, Md. 20910. Tel. (301) 589-1459

All ages.   Groups only.
Days & Hours: *By appointment.*
Admission: *Free.*
Guided Tour: *Telephone at least a few days in advance.*

NAVY ATHLETIC EVENTS

With the exception of varsity football, most sporting events in the Navy Marine Corps Memorial Stadium in Annapolis, Maryland, are free to the public.

For details inquire at the Visitors Information Center at Gate I, or write to the Navy Academy Athletic Association, Annapolis, Maryland 21402.

PUPPETS

Puppets are a favorite with the young set everywhere and Washington is no exception. In and around the capital puppet shows take place all year in museums, parks, and in cultural and recreational centers.

The following are a few of the many places where puppet performances are presented. For information call:

1. The Smithsonian   381-5395
2. National Capital Parks   426-6829
3. Glen Echo Park, Maryland   (301) 229-3031
4. Summer in the Park   426-6770
5. D.C. Recreation Department   629-7211
6. Wolf Trap Farm Park   (703) 938-3810

Performances are often listed in the newspapers. For last minute information Dial-A-Park 426-6975 or the Smithsonian special event number 737-8811.

SHAKESPEARE LIBRARY AND THEATRE

The world's finest collection of the works and times of the Bard of Avon is housed in the Folger Shakespeare Library.

Though the library's 200,000 books and 40,000 manuscripts are restricted to scholars, visitors can enjoy the full-scale Elizabethan public theatre, the model of the Globe Playhouse, and the changing exhibits of books, memorabilia, and Shakespearean paintings.

There are poetry readings, performances by the Folger Theatre Group, and occasional concerts.

Folger Shakespeare Library
201 E. Capitol Street, S.E.
Washington, D.C. 20003. Tel. 546-4800

All ages.   Individuals & groups.
Days & Hours: *Open daily 10:00–4:30. Closed holidays. Closed Sundays from Labor Day to April 15.*
Admission: *Free.*
Guided Tour: *For individuals and small groups, Monday at 1:00 and 2:00 P.M. Large groups must write or telephone 546-5370 two weeks in advance.*

SPORTS AND OTHER ACTIVITIES

Washington and the nearby suburban areas offer many year-round free or nominally priced sports activities and arts and crafts programs.

1. D.C. Recreation Department has programs ranging from archery to weight lifting. The programs include arts and crafts courses, amateur theatrical productions, concerts, opera, and ballet performances.

For information call 629-7226, or write to D.C. Recreation Department, 3149 16th Street, N.W., Washington, D.C. 20010.

The Department's bulletin, *Do You Know,* lists all of its activities. Subscription $1.00 a year.

2. The National Capital Parks Service conducts a full range of recreational and cultural activities, from free lunch hour concerts to hikes, talks, arts and crafts, drum lessons, and painting and sculpture workshops.

Dial-A-Park (426-6975) has up-to-date information on all park activities. And ask to be placed on the mailing list of their free monthly Calendar of Events. Write National Capital Parks, 1100 Ohio Drive, S.W., Washington, D.C. 20242, or telephone 426-6700.

3. The Maryland National Capital Park and Planning Commission operates a network of regional parks that offer a variety of leisure-time activities and facilities, including archery ranges, ice skating rinks, riding stables, and tennis courts.

For additional information contact one of the following:

Montgomery County Regional Headquarters
8787 Georgia Avenue
Silver Spring, Md. 20907. Tel. (301) 589-1480

Prince George's County Regional Headquarters
6600 Kenilworth Avenue
Riverdale, Md. 20840. Tel. (301) 277-2200

4. Annual expositions and sports events are held at:

1. Capital Centre
   Landover, Md. 20786. Tel. (301) 350-3400

2. Washington Coliseum
   M and 3rd Sts., N.E.
   Washington, D.C. 20002. Tel. 547-5800

3. National Guard Armory
   2001 East Capitol Street, N.E.
   Washington, D.C. 20003. Tel. 547-9077

4. Robert F. Kennedy Memorial Stadium
   East Capitol & 22nd St., N.E.
   Washington, D.C. 20003. Tel. 544-1900

See local newspapers for schedules.

WOLF TRAP FARM PARK FOR THE PERFORMING ARTS

Wolf Trap Farm Park in nearby Virginia is the first national park in the country dedicated to the performing arts. The 100-acre park has its own symphony orchestra and training program for future professionals. It also presents each summer leading orchestras, ballet companies, jazz musicians, and other performing artists of note.

Many programs are especially prepared for the enjoyment of young children, including the puppet shows in which live actors play the role of the characters.

Wolf Trap Farm (18 miles from D.C.)
1551 Trap Road
Vienna, Va. 22180. Tel. (703) 938-3810

All ages.   Individuals & groups.

Days & Hours: The park is open all year. Programs are from June to September.

Admission: Free to the park and to the children's programs, including puppet shows, but reservations to performances must be made in advance. For evening performances check newspapers for schedules and Box Office for tickets and prices. Tel. (703) 938-3800.

Guided Tour: By appointment. Telephone in advance.

9 Sea and Sky

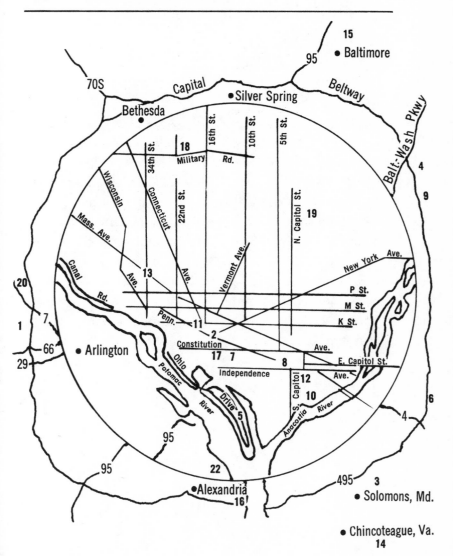

MAP LEGEND

1. Dulles International Airport
2. National Aquarium
3. Chesapeake Biological Laboratory
4. Goddard Space Flight Center
5. Lightship *Chesapeake*
6. Chesapeake Bay Maritime Museum
7. Smithsonian Museum of Natural History
8. National Air and Space Museum
9. U.S. Naval Academy
10. Navy Memorial Museum
11. Truxton-Decatur Naval Museum
12. U.S. Navy Combat Art Center
13. U.S. Naval Observatory
14. Oyster Museum
15. U.S. Frigate *Constellation*
16. U.S.S. *Laffey*
17. Smithsonian Museum of History and Technology
18. Rock Creek Nature Center Planetarium
19. Catholic University
20. Federal Aviation Administration
21. Three Springs Fisheries, Inc.
22. National Weather Service

AIRPORT

The Dulles International Airport is situated in Northern Virginia, 26 miles from the White House. The airport was specifically designed for jet planes and serves nine international airlines.

Sightseeing attractions here include the 600-foot-long terminal building and the 177-foot-high control tower.

The airport provides tours of its operations and activities, but to board an aircraft you must contact the airline of your choice.

Dulles International Airport (26 miles from D.C.)
Washington, D.C. 20041. Tel. (703) 471-7838

Ages 10 and up.   Groups only, but individuals may join scheduled tours.
Days & Hours: Monday–Friday, twice daily.
Admission: *Free.*
Guided Tour: *By appointment. Tours last about an hour. Write or telephone at least two days in advance.*

AQUARIUM

Sharks, octopuses, eyeless cave fish, and other strange and exotic species live here in the oldest aquarium in the country. Their home is the lower lobby of the Commerce Building, where seventy large tanks, some holding 2,500 gallons of water, display the various fish.

There are no guided tours, but exhibits are well documented, and the helpful staff is always nearby (in Room B-037) to answer questions.

A larger and more modern aquarium building is in the planning stages.

National Aquarium
Department of Commerce Building
14th Street and Constitution Avenue, N.W.
Washington, D.C. 20230. Tel. 967-2825

All ages.   Individuals & groups.
Days & Hours: Daily 9:00–5:00. Closed Christmas.
Admission: Free.
Guided Tour: Not available.

CHESAPEAKE BIOLOGICAL LABORATORY

The Chesapeake Biological Laboratory is engaged in research on life in the Chesapeake Bay area and on Maryland's natural resources.

Individually-tailored programs may be arranged for groups with special interests.

Chesapeake Biological Laboratory (65 miles from D.C.)
Solomons, Md. 20688. Tel. (301) 326-4281

All ages.   Individuals & groups.
Days & Hours: Monday–Friday 9:00–5:00.
Admission: Free.
Guided Tour: Groups should write or telephone two months
*   in advance.*

GODDARD SPACE FLIGHT CENTER

Youngsters of all ages with a keen interest in space travel tingle with excitement at the thought of a visit to NASA's Goddard Space Flight Center.

The tour begins with an orientation program, and includes a short film, exhibits of spacecraft, satellites, and documented displays of space-science equipment and technology.

Goddard Space Flight Center (8 miles from D.C.)
Greenbelt, Md. 20771. Tel. (301) 982-4101

Ages 9 and up.   Individuals & groups.
Days & Hours: Monday–Friday 10:00–2:00, but subject to change.
Admission: Free.
Guided Tour: Write or telephone one month in advance.

LIGHTSHIP

A lightship is a vessel with a bright light that patrols the shore and marks dangerous spots such as shoals or reefs. It also collects information on waves, tides, coastal currents, and temperatures at various sea depths.

The first lightship in the United States was operated in the Chesapeake Bay.

The "retired" lightship *Chesapeake* was recommissioned and is now used as a floating laboratory for visiting local students from elementary school through college age.

The lightship has an aquarium depicting life in the Potomac River, a fully operating weather station, and exhibits on water analysis and water cycles.

Lightship *Chesapeake*
Moored on the Potomac River at:
1200 Ohio Drive, S.W.
Washington, D.C. 20242. Tel. 426-6896/97

All ages.   Individuals & groups.
Days & Hours: *June–August: Tuesday, Thursday, and week-ends, 1:00–4:00. September–May: Only week-ends, 1:00–4:00.*
Admission: *Free.*
Guided Tour: *Available, but ship is frequently out of port. Check before you come.*

MARITIME MUSEUM

The Chesapeake Bay Maritime Museum collects, pre-serves, and exhibits artifacts and records pertaining to the sea. On display is a fine collection of models and relics of vessels used for fishing, oystering, and freighting in the Bay waters.

Lightship #79, built in 1904 and serving more than 63 years on active duty, is now part of the museum. It is open to tourists as well as sea scouts and other groups of young people who come here for marine study activities.

St. Michaels, home of the Maritime Museum, is a quaint old harbor town, rich in early American history. The story goes that the British planned to attack St. Michaels during the War of 1812 to destroy its shipyards. The town's residents found out about the scheme and on that fateful night hung lit lanterns high in the trees, the lights from a distance looking like windows. The British, believing the town to be on a high bank, shot over the roofs, leaving the town untouched.

St. Michaels is still remembered as "The Town That Fooled the British."

Chesapeake Bay Maritime Museum (80 miles from
   D.C.)
St. Michaels, Md. 21663. Tel. (301) 745-2916

All ages.   Individuals & groups.
Days & Hours: Summer: Open daily 10:00–5:00. Winter: Tuesday–Sunday 10:00–4:00. Closed Christmas.
Admission: Children: $.50. Adults: $1.50. Special group rates.
Guided Tour: By appointment. For large groups write or telephone two weeks in advance.

METEORITES

Some of the stony or metallic bodies that have plummeted down from outer space look like free-form sculptures.

If you like abstract art, you'll love this exhibit, and will learn about these once-heavenly bodies as well.

• At the Smithsonian Museum of Natural History.

NATIONAL AIR AND SPACE MUSEUM

A tour through the National Air and Space Museum is a glimpse into the history of man's attempt at flight.

Displays include the original Wright Brothers' plane, Charles Lindbergh's Spirit of St. Louis, a Lunar Landing Module of the type that landed the Apollo II astronauts on the moon, the moonrock, a mass of extraterrestrial matter from the moon, and many other historic aircraft and space vehicles.

Currently the collection is housed in the Arts and Industries and the nearby temporary Air and Space buildings, but the new National Air and Space Museum is now under construction and is scheduled to open during the Bicentennial in July 1976. It is expected to be one of the great aerospace centers of the world and is designed to provide a more expansive area for displays and research.

The address of the new museum is:

The Mall
Between 4th and 7th Streets, S.W.
Washington, D.C. 20560. Tel. 381-6264

• See Section on the Smithsonian.

NAVAL ACADEMY

Three hundred acres of land, two hundred buildings, and more than four thousand midshipmen make up this huge training center for U.S. Navy and Marine Corps officers.

Young visitors will enjoy watching the students line up in formation every hour in front of Bancroft Hall, the largest dormitory in the world, before marching to their next class.

Tourists can observe the colorful Brigade Noon Formation on the front terrace of Bancroft Hall: 12:05 P.M. weekdays; 12:10 P.M. Saturdays; 12:30 P.M. Sundays and holidays. There are also Dress Parades at 3:30 on Wednesday afternoons during spring and fall. All formations are subject to weather conditions.

The Academy Chapel holds the tomb of John Paul Jones, considered the father of the United States Navy. He is remembered for his famous battle cry, "I have not yet begun to fight!"

Visitors may explore the grounds on their own or join regularly scheduled tours. For information ask Visitors' Information Service at Gate I.

The Naval Academy Museum is located in Preble Hall, and houses a collection of more than 50,000 Navy-related items, including marine architecture, coins, costumes, seascapes, and the famous Roger Collection of ship models.

Also at the Academy is a bell brought from Okinawa by Commodore Matthew C. Perry in 1854. This bell is reputed to have been cast in 1456, and was named the "Japanese Bell" by a student at Annapolis.

United States Naval Academy (25 miles from D.C.)
Annapolis, Md. 21402. Tel. (301) 267-2291

All ages.   Individuals & groups.
*Days & Hours: Monday–Saturday 9:00–5:00. Sunday 12:00–5:00.
              Closed Christmas and New Year's.*
Admission: Free.
*Guided Tour: Scheduled daily May–October. Adults: $1.00.
              Children under 7 free.*

NAVAL HISTORY

1. More than 4,000 Navy-related historic objects are on display at the Navy Memorial Museum. Ship models, paintings, photographs, and weapons ranging from cannons to replicas of the first atomic bomb are here. Of special interest is President Kennedy's collection of ship models and the submarine room with three operating periscopes where children view the surrounding areas.

Tanks, midget submarines, and missiles are on the outside grounds.

Navy Memorial Museum
Building 76
Washington Navy Yard
Washington, D.C. 20374. Tel. 433-2651

All ages.   Individuals & groups.
*Days & Hours: Monday–Friday 9:00–4:00. Weekends and holi-
              days 10:00–5:00.*
Admission: Free.
Guided Tour: For special groups or occasions only.

2. The Truxton-Decatur Naval Museum, operated by the Naval Historical Foundation, has displays of ship models, paintings of naval heroes and battles, wheels, clocks, helms, and other equipment from historic vessels.

Truxton-Decatur Naval Museum
1610 H Street, N.W.
Washington, D.C. 20006. Tel. 783-2573

All ages.   Individuals & groups.
Days & Hours: Daily 10:30–4:00. Closed holidays.
Admission: Free.
Guided Tour: Not available.

3. Artists have recorded the story of naval and marine units at sea and ashore, in war and in peace, since before World War II. Military action, launchings, explorations, and sailings have often been captured on canvas. These paintings are exhibited at the U.S. Navy Combat Art Center.

Artists continue to record and interpret their impressions of the Navy and the men who serve her. Each year the collection increases by approximately 150 canvases.

Changing exhibits are on display all year.

U.S. Navy Combat Art Center
Building 67
Washington Navy Yard
Washington, D.C. 20374. Tel. 433-3816

All ages.   Individuals & groups.
Days & Hours: Daily 8:00–4:00. Closed holidays.
Admission: Free.
Guided Tour: Not available.

NAVAL OBSERVATORY

One of the most famous observatories in the world is also the Navy's oldest scientific institution.

Established in 1830 in a small office to maintain chronometers, charts, and other navigational equipment, it now occupies a complex of 50 buildings on 72 acres of land.

Among its many functions, the observatory measures time, so vital in sea and space travel and in scientific research. Its master clock, accurate within one one-millionth of a second per day, is the nation's authoritative timekeeping instrument.

U.S. Naval Observatory
Massachusetts Avenue at 34th Street, N.W.
Washington, D.C. 20390. Tel. 254-4533

Ages 12 and up.   Individuals & groups. 1 adult to 10 children.
Days & Hours: *See below.*
Admission: *Free.*
Guided Tour: *Tour starts at 2:00 P.M., Monday–Friday. Closed holidays. Large groups should write one month in advance to Superintendent, U.S. Naval Observatory, at the above address.*

OYSTER MUSEUM

It's far from Washington, but if you're in the area, be sure to visit the Oyster Museum, the only one of its kind in the country. On display are shell exhibits, farming instruments, and ship models, as well as bird, animal, and marine life in the area. The museum also has a library that specializes in marine life.

Oyster Museum of Chincoteague (150 miles from D.C.)
P.O. Box 14
Chincoteague, Va. 23336. Tel. (804) 336-6117

All ages.   Individuals & groups.
Days & Hours: Open daily May 30–August 30, 11:00–5:00 and on weekends from September through November. Closed December to March 30, but special groups may arrange visits.
Admission: Children: $.25.   Adults: $.50.
Guided Tour: By appointment. Write or telephone two weeks in advance.

SHIPS

1. The U.S. Frigate *Constellation,* known as the "Yankee Racehorse," is the nation's elder warship. Launched in 1797, it fought pirates in Tripoli, Libya, in 1802, saw action in the War of 1812, and is the oldest surviving fighting vessel of the Civil War.

Today it is a museum-ship berthed in the Baltimore harbor not far from Ft. McHenry where Francis Scott Key wrote "The Star-Spangled Banner."

U.S. Frigate *Constellation* (40 miles from D.C.)
Pier 1, Pratt Street
Baltimore, Md. 21202. Tel. (301) 539-1797

Ages 6 and up.   Individuals & groups.

Days & Hours: *May–Labor Day, weekdays 10:00–6:00, Sundays & holidays 12:00–6:00. Other times, weekdays 10:00–4:00, Sundays & holidays 12:00–5:00. Closed Christmas, New Year's, and Good Friday.*

Admission: *Children under 12: $.50. Adults: $1.50. Special group rates.*

Guided Tour: *On weekends, every other hour. Large groups, write or telephone in advance.*

2. The U.S.S. *Laffey* is a historic destroyer which fought in the Korean and Second World wars. It is now berthed in Alexandria, Virginia.

U.S.S. *Laffey*

Franklin Street Pier

Alexandria, Va. 22314. Tel. (703) 274-7979

All ages.   Groups only.

Days & Hours: *By appointment.*

Admission: *Free.*

Guided Tour: *Write or telephone one to two weeks in advance.*

3. Sailors and landlubbers alike will enjoy this huge collection of ship models. The vessels range from a 9th-century Viking ship to tugboats, ships-of-war, and ocean liners, including the *Mayflower* and the *Santa María*. Other exhibits feature navigational instruments, sailmaking, and ship designing.

• At the Smithsonian Museum of History and Technology.

STARS

1. In a 45-minute show, a projector illuminates the 24-foot dome with images of celestial bodies while a park naturalist explains the movement of the stars.

Rock Creek Nature Center Planetarium
Military & Glover Roads, N.W.
Washington, D.C. 20015. Tel. 426-6829.

Ages 7 and up.	Individuals & groups.
Shows:	*Wednesday & Friday, 4:00 P.M. Saturday, 10:00 A.M. and 2:00 P.M. Special show for children 4–7, Sunday, 1:15.*
Admission:	*Free.*
Guided Tour:	*Consists of a lecture on the stars. Visits may be arranged for groups during school hours.*

2. The National Capital Astronomers Club meets in Rock Creek Park opposite St. John's High School, once a month from May through October. Admission is free. For more information call 426-6829.

TORNADOES

Catholic University's Department of Aerospace and Atmospheric Sciences houses the only tornado-producing laboratory in the United States. Here scientists and students investigate and study the forecasting, control, and modification of this violent, sometimes destructive windstorm.

Encased in a 10 × 3 foot cylindrical chamber with "windows," the tornado can be observed as it generates, matures, decays, and subsides. Members of the staff explain how to improve safety precautions of an area against a tornado and what to do when a storm does hit.

The Catholic University of America
620 Michigan Avenue, N.E.
Washington, D.C. 20017. Tel. 635-5163

Ages 16 and up.   Groups of 10–20 persons.
Days & Hours: Monday–Friday 9:00–5:00.
Admission: Free.
Guided Tour: Telephone two to three weeks in advance.

TRAFFIC IN THE AIR

The Federal Aviation Administration uses radar, computers, and other sophisticated electronic equipment to control the traffic flow caused by 1,300,000 aircraft operations each year.

A regular tour of the FAA's Washington Air Route Traffic Control Center gives youngsters the chance to observe radarscopes in operation, to listen to air-to-ground communications, and to learn how air-control specialists keep traffic moving safely in the skies.

Federal Aviation Administration
Washington Air Route Traffic Control Center (40
    miles from D.C.)
Virginia Route #7

Leesburg, Va. 22110. Tel. (703) 777-4400, (202) 783-
0745

Ages 8 and up. Individuals & groups.
Days & Hours: By appointment.
Admission: Free.
Guided Tour: Write or telephone one week in advance.

TREASURES OF THE SEA

Ever since man first began to sail the oceans, he has lost
men, ships, and untold treasures.

Scientists have long hoped to locate the treasures and
to recover them from the bottom of the sea.

The Hall of Underwater Exploration houses the tools
men use for these efforts, and features an exciting exhibit
of uniformed divers searching the seabed and some of the
sunken treasures they have uncovered.

• At the Smithsonian Museum of History and Technology.

TROPICAL FISH

Three Springs Fisheries is one of the country's largest
producers of goldfish, from the newly hatched little ones
to mature adults over one foot long.

In addition, an assortment of tropical fish, aquatic birds,
varied water lily plants, and other flora can also be seen.

Three Springs Fisheries, Inc. (38 miles from D.C.)
Lilypons, Md. 21717. Tel. (301) 874-5133

Ages 5 and up.   Individuals & groups.
Days & Hours: *Monday–Saturday 9:00–3:00. Sunday 1:00–3:00.*
                      Closed September–March and Easter Sunday.
Admission: *Free.*
Guided Tour: *Not available.*

WEATHER BUREAU

Those with a special interest in meteorology will receive an explanation on the workings of the Weather Bureau by a staff member.

Group tours are scheduled on Tuesday and Thursday, but up to three persons are welcome any day if they notify the Meteorologist In Charge (MIC) in advance.

National Weather Service (1½ miles from D.C.)
Washington National Airport
Washington, D.C. 20001. Tel. (703) 557-2648

Ages 10 and up.   Individuals & groups.
Days & Hours: *Open all year, but tours are on Tuesday and Thursday at 10:00.*
Admission: *Free.*
Guided Tour: *Groups should make arrangements two to three weeks in advance.*

10 Other Lands

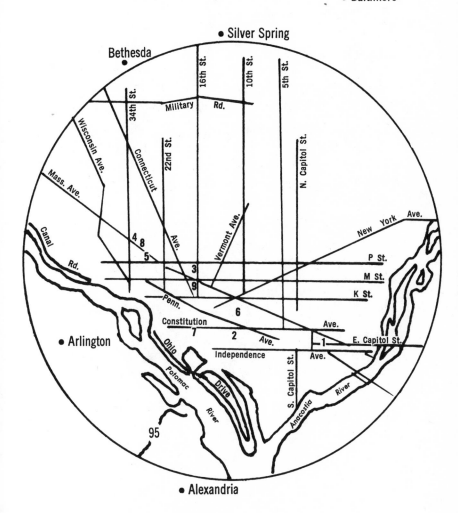

MAP LEGEND

1. Museum of African Art
2. Smithsonian Museum of Natural History
3. Embassy of Australia
4. Imperial Embassy of Iran
5. Embassy of Japan
6. Safeway International Supermarket
7. House of the Americas
8. The Islamic Center
9. National Geographic Society

AFRICAN ART

A unique collection of African art, crafts, and musical instruments is on exhibit here.

Visitors are permitted to handle many of the art objects and may try on African robes and play authentic native musical instruments. Instruction is given in traditional African songs, dances, and games.

Tours are tailored to individual groups.

Museum of African Art
316–318 A Street, N.E.
Washington, D.C. 20002. Tel. 547-7424

All ages.   Individuals & groups.
Days & Hours: *Monday–Friday 11:00–5:00. Saturday & Sunday 12:30–5:00.*
Admission: *Suggested contribution: Children: $.25.   Adults: $.50.*
Guided Tour: *Lasts about one hour. For group tours, telephone at least one week in advance.*

CRAFTS

Ivory carvings, wampum belts, a crown of feathers, Malaysian shadow puppets, and other handmade crafts and art objects can be seen in the Smithsonian's Cultures of Africa and Asia and Cultures of the Pacific and Asia exhibits, located on the first floor of the Smithsonian Museum of Natural History.

In addition, there is a collection of musical instruments

where visitors may press a button to hear tribal rhythms and to see a slide show of these instruments being played. As with all such instruments, these sound makers not only serve to create music but to send signals to tribesmen near and far.

EMBASSIES

A visit to a foreign embassy provides a glimpse into the lives of other lands and cultures, and some embassies welcome visitors, individuals, and class groups free of charge the year round.

Each spring a number of embassies open their doors to the public to benefit worthy causes, and thousands visit them.

By previous arrangement the following embassies may be visited:

1. The Australian Embassy. Visit the embassy of the only continent occupied by a single nation and enjoy a talk on Australian life and its people. The changing exhibits of Australia's arts and crafts are of interest to all ages.

Embassy of Australia
1601 Massachusetts Avenue, N.W.
Washington, D.C. 20036. Tel. 797-3172

Ages 12 and up.   Individuals & groups.
Days & Hours: By appointment.
Admission: Free.
Guided Tour: Write as far in advance as possible.

NOTE: *Young children with parents are welcome, but elementary school classes cannot be accommodated.*

2. Iranian Embassy. A visit to the Imperial Embassy of Iran is a delightful experience. It has beautifully tiled walls, magnificent carpets, and outstanding examples of Persian art.

Don't miss the Tent Room, which gives a glimpse into tribal life of Iran.

Imperial Embassy of Iran
3005 Massachusetts Avenue, N.W.
Washington, D.C. 20008. Tel. 483-5500, Ext. 36

Ages 12 and up.   Groups only.
Days & Hours: By appointment.
Admission: Free.
Guided Tour: Write two weeks in advance to Ms. Mariam
                  Dargahi, public relations.

3. Japanese Embassy. The Embassy of Japan welcomes tourists to visit the "Ippakutei," the name for the Japanese Ceremonial Tea House and Garden.

A guide will explain the origin of the Tea Ceremony, a semi-religious, social custom going back to the 15th century, but don't expect to be served tea or see a demonstration of the Tea Ceremony.

Embassy of Japan
2520 Massachusetts Avenue, N.W.
Washington, D.C. 20008. Tel. 234-2266, Ext. 310

Ages 11 and up.   Groups up to 30 people.

Guided Tour: *Wednesday afternoons from May through October. Closed August. Write two weeks in advance.*

FOOD AROUND THE WORLD

Safeway International, reputed to be the largest store of its kind in the world, is filled with a variety of cheeses and a wide assortment of gourmet foods ranging from antelope steak to Żubrowka, the Polish vodka.

The store sponsors national food festivals, and holds lecture programs and guided tours. Visitors are welcome to browse on their own through their favorite sections.

Safeway International Supermarket
1110 F Street, N.W.
Washington, D.C. 20004. Tel. 628-1880

Ages 5 and up.   Individuals & groups.
Days & Hours: Regular business hours.
Admission: Free.
Guided Tour: *Tuesday at 10:15 A.M., except holidays. Tele-
phone Ms. Arlette, Gourmetician, for appoint-
ment two months in advance.*

HOUSE OF THE AMERICAS

The Pan American Organization, now called the Organization of American States (OAS), was founded in 1890, and is the oldest international association in the world.

Its membership consists of 24 countries of the Western Hemisphere united to maintain peace, promote better understanding, and advance the welfare of the Americas.

The organization is housed in an impressive structure that contains an Aztec Garden, a Tropical Patio with a sliding glass roof, and an unusual collection of plants.

Here you can see a date palm tree, a banana plant, a coffee tree, and a "peace" tree.

Colorful Guatemalan macaws with their luscious plumage, as well as changing exhibits by artists of the Americas, are some of the other attractions.

House of the Americas
Organization of the American States Headquarters
17th Street & Constitution Avenue, N.W.
Washington, D.C. 20006. Tel. 393-8450

Ages 10 and up. Individuals & groups.
Days & Hours: Monday–Saturday 8:30–4:30.
Admission: Free.
Guided Tour: By appointment. Fee: $.15. Write to Visitors'
*   Service Department a few weeks in advance.*

ISLAM IN AMERICA

Built at an angle facing in the direction of the Holy City of Mecca, the Islamic Center is the largest mosque in the United States.

Its minaret (from the Arabic "manārah," lamp or lighthouse) is a 160-foot-high, slender tower with several balconies from which the "prayer caller" or muezzin summons the faithful to worship.

The inside of the mosque is covered with richly decorated tiled walls and priceless Persian carpets.

Believers and non-believers may attend services on the Moslem day of prayer, Friday at noon, and hear a short explanation of the worship.

Shoes must be removed before entering the mosque.

The Islamic Center
2551 Massachusetts Avenue, N.W.
Washington, D.C. 20008. Tel. 332-3451/7666

All ages.   Individuals & groups.
Days & Hours: Daily 10:00–4:00.
Admission: Free.
Guided Tour: By appointment. For group tours, write or telephone in advance. Individuals may join a group tour.

NATIONAL GEOGRAPHIC

The Explorers Hall of the National Geographic Society features exciting, authoritative exhibits of near and faraway lands, peoples, and expeditions.

A favorite attraction is the giant globe, measuring 11 feet in diameter and weighing 1,100 pounds.

The often-changed exhibits are authentic, instructive, and brilliantly presented.

Inquire about evening lectures.

National Geographic Society
17th & M Sts., N.W.
Washington, D.C. 20036. Tel. 296-7500, Ext. 527

All ages.   Individuals & groups.
Days & Hours: Monday–Friday 9:00–6:00, Saturday 9:00–5:00.
 Sunday 12:00–5:00.
Admission: Free.
Guided Tour: Not available. Large groups should write or telephone two weeks in advance.

11 Once a Year

ANNUAL EVENTS

To verify dates see the *Washington Post,* other local newspapers, or call the Washington Area Convention and Visitors Bureau, 1129 20th Street, N.W., Washington, D.C. 20036. Telephone 659-6400.

January
Every four years, on January 20th, a new President is inaugurated.

Recreation Vehicle Sports Camping Travel Show, Armory.*

Ice Show, Capital Centre.

February
Chinese New Year.

Washington International Boat Show, Armory.

March
Kite Carnival (mid-March or early April). See "Kite Flying," Chapter 8.

Egg Rolling (Monday after Easter Sunday), White House lawn.

Circus (late March or early April through May), Armory.

National Capital Kennel Club, Armory.

World on Wheels (last week in March), Armory.

---

* For a listing of exhibition halls, sports arenas and their locations, see "Sports and Other Activities," chapter eight.

April
Cherry Blossom Festival (late March or early April).
Circus America, Capital Centre.
Washington Redskins, RFK Stadium (April–October).

May
Rodeo, Capital Centre.
Lacrosse (May–July), Capital Centre.
Boomerang Competition (May or June). See "Boomeranging," Chapter 8.

June
President's Cup Regatta, Potomac River.
Festival of American Life (end of June and early July), on the Mall.

July
Independence Day Celebration (July 4th).

September
International Children's Day (mid-September). See "Wolf Trap Farm Park," Chapter 8.
Ice Show, Capital Centre.

October
Washington International Horse Show, Armory.
N.H.L. Hockey, Capital Centre (October–April).
N.B.A. Basketball, Capital Centre (October–April).
Jousting. See "Jousting," Chapter 8.

November
Mid-Atlantic Ski and Winter Sports Show, Armory.

December
Christmas Pageant of Peace, on the Ellipse.

Index

Note: Italicized entries are exhibits at the Smithsonian Institution.